1106530?o

CULTURAL PLURALISM IN EDUCATION:
A MANDATE FOR CHANGE

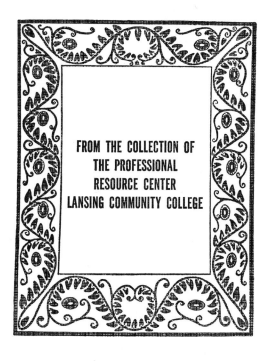

FROM THE COLLECTION OF
THE PROFESSIONAL
RESOURCE CENTER
LANSING COMMUNITY COLLEGE

CULTURAL PLURALISM IN EDUCATION: A Mandate for Change

MADELON D. STENT
The City College of New York (CUNY)

WILLIAM R. HAZARD
Northwestern University

HARRY N. RIVLIN
Fordham University

Professional Resource Center
LANSING COMMUNITY COLLEGE

Prentice-Hall, Inc., Englewood Cliffs, N. J.

Copyright © 1973 by Fordham University.
All rights reserved.

Copyright is claimed until 1978. Thereafter all portions of this work covered by this copyright will be in the public domain.

This work was developed under a contract from the U.S. Office of Education, Department of Health, Education and Welfare. However, the content does not necessarily reflect the position or policy of that Agency, and no official endorsement of these materials should be inferred.

No part of this book may be reproduced in any form or by any means, without permission in writing from the publisher, Prentice-Hall, Inc., Englewood Cliffs, N.J.

Printed in the United States of America

ISBN: 0-13-195461-X

Library of Congress Catalog Card Number: 72-92109

10 9 8 7 6 5 4 3 2 1

PRENTICE-HALL INTERNATIONAL, INC., *London*
PRENTICE-HALL OF AUSTRALIA, PTY. LTD., *Sydney*
PRENTICE-HALL OF CANADA, LTD., *Toronto*
PRENTICE-HALL OF INDIA PRIVATE LIMITED, *New Delhi*
PRENTICE-HALL OF JAPAN, INC., *Tokyo*

LANSING COMMUNITY COLLEGE LIBRARY

CONTENTS

PREFACE

The Cuban writer Jesus Castellanos once remarked that it is to be expected that a man should love the region in which he was born, but that that was no reason for hating those who were born elsewhere. Similarly, it is understandable that a person should respect and love the culture into which he was born and in which he has been brought up, but that is no reason for despising or hating the culture into which other people have been born.

One of the most difficult words for people to understand when they look at various cultures or sub-cultures is *different*. *Different* means *different*; it does not mean *better than* or *worse than*. This whole-hearted acceptance of one's own culture and of other people's culture is basic to the development of a sense of cultural pluralism that is far more enriching than is the outworn concept of the melting pot.

No child should have to feel that he must reject his parents' culture to be accepted. Indeed, his chances of adjusting successfully to his school, to his community, and to the larger society are enhanced if he is not encumbered by feelings of shame and of inferiority because he was not born into another family and another culture. To speak of any child as "culturally disadvantaged" merely because of his ethnic origin is damaging not only to the child but also to society, for it deprives the nation of the contributions that can be made by each of the many groups that make up our country.

Dewey's famous dictum that what the best and wisest of fathers wants for his child, that the state should want for all its children, has special significance today, for we stress the word *all*. By *all,* we mean *all*—the rich, the poor, the Whites, the Blacks, the Puerto Ricans, the American Indians, the Chicanos, the Chinese, and all the other ethnic groups in the United States.

In any program that aims at dealing with urban school problems and opportunities, pride of race is important but racism is vicious, whether it be expressed in discriminatory actions or in objectionable epithets or comments. As American citizens, especially as American educators working in urban communities, we must make every effort to stamp out racism and its manifestations, for racism is corrosive to all students and damages the learning process.

Harry N. Rivlin

[vii

CONTRIBUTORS

ARAGON, JOHN. Dr. Aragon is currently the director of the Minority Groups Cultural Awareness Center at the University of New Mexico, a department of the College of Education which works with community leaders, school administrators, and teachers to make public schools more responsive to the cultural diversity exhibited by their students. In addition to wide experience in New Mexico's school affairs, having served as a staff member of its Educational Association and as the first full-time executive secretary of its School Boards Association, Dr. Aragon has served on the National Education Association's Committee of International Education. This committee developed a program which provided United States educators to train teachers for those countries which requested such assistance. Dr. Aragon served as chief administrator of a U.S. AID program in Ecuador which developed a free textbook program, improved training for elementary teachers, and constructed 3,000 classrooms.

CLASBY, MIRIAM. Dr. Clasby is currently a Washington Intern in Education assigned to Dr. Don Davies' staff. After teaching at the college level in the United States and Japan, she directed an experimental urban education center in Roxbury, Massachusetts. While completing her doctoral studies at the Harvard Graduate School of Education, she also served as chairman of the Editorial Board of the *Harvard Educational Review.*

DAVIES, DON. Dr. Davies is Deputy Commissioner for Development, Office of Education. His conviction that the reform of American education requires the development of alternatives to traditional schooling derives from extensive experience with teacher education. After completing his baccalaureate and masters at Stanford University and a doctorate at Columbia Teachers College, Dr. Davies was a member of the faculties of Adelphi College, San Francisco State College, and the University of Minnesota, directly involved in student teaching. Later he served as executive secretary of the National Education Association's National Commission on Teacher Education and Professional Standards and vice-chairman of the President's National Advisory Council on Education Professions Department. In 1968 he became Associate Commissioner for Educational Personnel Development with the Office of Education. Dr. Davies has published a number of studies and articles on improving teacher education, student teaching, and teacher development.

DELORIA, VINE, JR. Mr. Deloria is an enrolled member of the Standing Rock Sioux Tribe, Fort Yates, North Dakota. Following service in the U.S. Marine Corps (1954-1956), Mr. Deloria received degrees at Iowa State University (B.S., 1958), Lutheran School of Theology (B.D., 1963), and the University of Colorado School of Law (J.D., 1970). As staff associate, United Scholarship Service (1963-1964), he developed a secondary schools placement program for American Indian students. He has served as Executive Director, National Congress of American Indians (1965-1967), and is currently president of the Institute for the Development of Indian Law, a new organization to work on the legal problems of the American Indian. His two recent books, *Custer Died for Your Sins* and *We Talk, You Listen*, received overwhelming critical acclaim.

DOUGLASS, MALCOLM P. Dr. Douglass is Professor of Education and Director of the new Claremont Center for Developmental Studies in Education at the Claremont Graduate School, one of the Claremont Colleges situated in Southern California. For several years he has directed the Claremont Reading Conference and edited its annual yearbook. His central interest is in the problem of achieving adequate levels of literacy.

FRASER, DOROTHY M. Dr. Fraser is professional assistant to the Director of the Training the Teacher Trainers-Leadership Training Institute (TTT LTI) and Professor of Education, Hunter College of the City University of New York. Dr. Fraser earned the B.S. in Education from Northeastern Missouri State College at Kirksville, the M.A. from the University of Missouri, and the Ph.D. from the University of Minnesota. Working in the field of social studies education, she has taught in public schools in Missouri and at the University of Minnesota High School, the University of Chicago Laboratory School, and The City College of the City University of New York. She served as social studies specialist in the U.S. Office of Education, and is a past president of the National Council for the Social Studies. Dr. Fraser was involved in the TTT Program during its beginning stages, as director of the Northeastern Regional TTT Institute, and has served as professional assistant to the Director of the TTT LTI since 1970.

GUERRA, MANUEL H.   Dr. Guerra is presently teaching at the Stanford University Chicano Seminar. A specialist in bilingual education and Spanish language and literature, he was awarded the Presidential Citation and bronze medal for his bilingual and bicultural studies concerning Mexican-American children. He holds the B.A. degree from the University of Wisconsin and the Ph.D. from the University of Michigan. Dr. Guerra has served as lecturer on bilingual education at Stanford University, as a consultant for Title I, as chairman of the Education Counsel of the Mexican-American Political Association, as specialist on bilingual education in the State Education Department of California, as Community-Counselor for Mecha students in California. His other teaching experience has included six years at the State University of New York, Buffalo, five years at the University of Southern Califronia, and work as Professor of Ethnic Studies and Bilingual Education, Washington State University. He is the author of "Educating Chicano Children and Youths," which appeared in the January 1972 issue of the *Phi Delta Kappan*, and his latest book is *Essays: Mexican-Americans in Education*, published by the Valley Forge Press.

HARDING, VINCENT.   Dr. Harding is Director of the Institute of the Black World, an independent research center in Atlanta. Until recently (September 1, 1970), the Institute was a part of the Martin Luther King, Jr. Memorial Center. Prior to his work with the Institute and the Center, Dr. Harding was chairman of the History and Sociology Department at Spelman College in Atlanta for four years. Born in New York City in 1931, he attended public schools there and received his college and university training from The City College of New York, (B.A., 1952) Columbia University (M.S., 1953) and the University of Chicago (M.A., 1956 and Ph.D., 1965). Dr. Harding is married and has two children. He has published and lectured widely, and is currently working on several books on the Black Experience.

HATA, DON, JR.   Dr. Hata is Assistant Professor of History, Chairman of the East Asian Interdepartmental Program, and Director of the Asian American Research Project at California State College, Dominguez Hills. Born in East Los Angeles in 1939, a fourth generation American, he was an inmate of the United States War Relocation Authority concentration camp at Gila, Arizona, 1942-1943. Dr. Hata earned his Ph.D. at the University of Southern California and has served as Visiting Instructor in Far Eastern History at Occidental College. He is married to Nadine Iku Ishitani.

HAZARD, WILLIAM R. Dr. Hazard, who served as cochairman of the Chicago conference on Education and Teacher Education for Cultural Pluralism, is Associate Dean and Professor, School of Education, Northwestern University. In addition, he is the director of Northwestern University's TTT project and the director of the TTT Midwest Cluster. A practicing attorney, Dean Hazard has conducted research, written, and taught in the areas of teacher-board relations, teacher education, and school law. His two most recent books are *Education and the New Teacher* (co-authored with B. J. Chandler and Daniel Powell) and *Education and the Law: Cases and Materials on Public Schools.*

PLATERO, DILLON. Mr. Platero is Director of Rough Rock Demonstration School, Chinle, Arizona. He is a Navajo Indian and was the founder and first editor of the *Navajo Times.* Mr. Platero has also been the chairman of the Navajo Tribal Education Committee, and Field Director of the Indian Community Action Project at Arizona State University for the states of Florida, North Carolina, Mississippi, and Colorado. He is a member of the National Advisory Committee on Bilingual Education.

RIVLIN, HARRY N. Dr. Rivlin is the Dean of the Fordham University School of Education, which has reorganized all of its programs for the preparation of educational personnel so that they now focus on the opportunities and the problems of urban education. Prior to his present appointment, he was University Dean of Teacher Education for the City University of New York. He is the Director of TTT LTI and was first a member of and then a consultant to the NDEA Institute for Advanced Study in Teaching Disadvantaged Youth. He was a member of the New York City School-Community Committee for Educational Excellence, which drafted the report leading to New York City's adoption of an Apprentice Teacher Program. He was chairman of the New York State Regents Advisory Board on Teacher Education, Certification, and Practice. He has also been active in various national organizations and programs, as indicated by his service as a member of the National Commission on Teacher Education and Professional Standards of the National Education Association and as a coordinator for the Great Cities School Improvement Program.

SEDA BONILLA, EDUARDO. Dr. Seda Bonilla is the Director of the Puerto Rican Studies program at Hunter College of the City University of New York. In addition to his award-winning report on the civic culture of Puerto Rico, he has contributed to a generation of Puerto Rican studies with his many original ideas, such as the operational steps involved in the concept of power as a factor in the socialization of personality in society. A generation of young students at the University of Puerto Rico, Columbia University, New York University, and City University have benefited from his teaching. His latest book is *Requiem for a Culture.*

SEKAQUAPTEWA, EUGENE. Mr. Sekaquaptewa is Education Programs Administrator for the Hopi tribe at the Hopi Indian Agency, Keams Canyon, Arizona. He was born and attended elementary and high school on the Hopi Indian Reservation in Arizona and later earned the degree of B.S. in Education and the M.A. in Counseling from Arizona State University, Tempe, Arizona. He served in the rank of Captain with the U.S. Air Force, Security Service. He has taught for the Bureau of Indian Affairs at schools on and off Indian reservations. Prior to his present position, Mr. Sekaquaptewa served as Assistant Professor of Education at Arizona State University, teaching Indian education courses and pursuing a graduate degree in school supervision.

SIZEMORE, BARBARA A. Mrs. Sizemore is the Coordinator for Proposal Development in the Department of Government Funded Programs, Chicago Public Schools, and former Director-District Superintendent of the Woodlawn Experimental Schools District, a Title III project. Since earning her B.A. in Latin from Northwestern in 1947, she has been a classroom teacher, an elementary and a high school principal, an instructor at Northeastern Illinois State College's Center for Inner City Studies, and a staff associate at the Midwest Administration Center of the University of Chicago, where she is currently working toward her doctorate in educational administration, with emphasis on the mobilization of community control. She has served as consultant to many local and out-of-state programs, such as the Cincinnati School Survey, the Head Start Follow-Through Project, the National Association of State School Boards, the Black Sisters Conference, and the U.S. Office of Education.

SMALLEY, MARY JANE. Dr. Smalley is Chief, Site Planning and Development Branch, Northeast Division, National Center for the Improvement of Educational Systems, Office of Education. After completing her B.A. at Southwestern at Memphis and her M.A. at Radcliffe, Dr. Smalley earned the Ph.D. degree at Harvard University. Before joining the Office of Education in 1967, she served as a Teaching Fellow at Harvard and a member of the faculty at Wellesley College. Dr. Smalley's responsibilities in the Office of Education have included work in the Foreign Language

Institute Program and the Basic Studies Program as well as continuing association since its inception with the Program for Training the Trainers of Teachers, in which she served as Acting Chief and Chief from 1970 to 1972.

SMITH, WILLIAM L.   Dr. Smith is the Acting Associate Commissioner, National Center for the Improvement of Educational Systems, Office of Education. Earning his baccalaureate at Wiley College in Marshall, Texas, his master's degree at Massachusetts State Teachers College in Boston, and his doctorate at Case Western Reserve University, Dr. Smith brings to his present assignment a varied background of experience as a teacher, a social worker, a counselor, a school administrator, and the director of the PACE Association, an independent organization which promoted educational innovations in 32 greater Cleveland public school districts. He has chaired numerous educational committees and commissions, such as the Education Subcommittee of the Mayor's Council on Youth Opportunities in Cleveland and the Curriculum Review and Evaluation Committee of the Cleveland Public Schools. Since joining the Office of Education in 1969, Dr. Smith has served in leadership roles in the Career Opportunities Program, Division of School Programs, the Teacher Corps Program, and the Bureau of Educational Personnel Development. In March 1972, he was named Educator of the Year by Case Western Reserve University Graduate School Alumni Association and by Phi Delta Kappa.

STENT, MADELON D.   Dr. Stent, who is an associate professor at The City College of the City University of New York (serving as the director of the TTT program and Visiting Associate Professor at Fordham University while on leave of absence from the City University) was the cochairman of the Conference on Education and Teacher education for Cultural Pluralism. Dr. Stent is president and founder of Urban Ed, Inc., the first minority based educational consultative corporation in the United States. In addition to her many research and community activities, Dr. Stent was one of the originators and authors of the highly successful biweekly children's reading paper *New York, New York,* published by Random House.

TYSON, CYRIL D.   Mr. Tyson is Vice-President of Optimum Computer Systems, Inc. He was formerly a Teaching Fellow at the John F. Kennedy School of Government, Institute of Politics, and Research Associate at the Program on Technology and Society of Harvard University. He also served as the Deputy Administrator—Commissioner of the Human Resources

Administration Manpower and Career Development Agency of New York City, where he developed the first Comprehensive Manpower System. Mr. Tyson is past Executive Director of the United Community Corporation, the community action agency for the City of Newark, New Jersey and was Executive Director of Haryou-Act Inc. in Central Harlem. He was Project Director of the unique study *Youth In The Ghetto: A Study of the Consequences of Powerlessness and a Blueprint for Change* published by Harlem Youth Opportunities Unlimited. He served on a study mission for the American Jewish Committee to assess the applicability of Israel's techniques for solving its problems of poverty and cultural lag to similar problems that isolate large segments of our population from the main stream of American life.

CULTURAL PLURALISM IN EDUCATION: A MANDATE FOR CHANGE

1

EDUCATION AND TEACHER EDUCATION FOR CULTURAL PLURALISM

HARRY N. RIVLIN AND DOROTHY M. FRASER

Having a diversity of cultures within a single country can be a threat, a problem, or an asset. The purpose of the Conference on Education and Teacher Education for Cultural Pluralism, which was held in Chicago on May 12-14, 1971, was to take steps to make the cultural diversity that characterizes American society a major asset instead of being a problem or becoming a threat. So important a purpose as this cannot be achieved by mere talk, even by persuasive talk by informed and eloquent people. For this reason, the major emphasis of the conference was focused on the recommendations for action that were to come from the participants and on plans for translating these recommendations into actuality.

The Conference on Education and Teacher Education for Cultural Pluralism was deliberately structured to lead to recommendations for action. The basic theme and the general structure of the conference were set at an early meeting of the Conference Planning Committee, where it had the good fortune to be joined by several most helpful BEPD[1] staff

---

[1] While we may disagree on the importance of learning the alphabet as a first step in learning to read, there is no gainsaying the importance of knowing what letters stand for when we try to understand the structure and functioning of education today.

If the reader is to follow what is said below while the editors stay within space limitations, all should know the following abbreviations:

members: Rosemarie Brooks, Charles Foster, Bruce Gaarder, Alfreda Lieberman, Anne Meers, Shirley Radcliffe, Allen Schmieder, Mary Jane Smalley, Stewart Tinsman, and Donald Tuttle.

It was agreed that there would be eight discussion groups, each of which would be so organized as to assure its having some participants from each of the four parity groups: community, liberal arts, schools, and teacher education. Each group was to have a presenter who would develop his views on a particular aspect of cultural pluralism in a paper that would be sent, in advance of the conference, to participants assigned to that group. Provided with a chairman and a reactor to start the discussion, each group was to formulate a series of recommendations for action, with the assurance that each recommendation would be submitted to the person or agency most likely to be able to implement it.

Though the Conference Planning Committee could assure numerical parity among the four parity groups by inviting an equal number of participants from each and by assigning equal numbers to each discussion group, more had to be done to assure parity of influence in the formulation of recommendations for action. For one thing, some of the community representatives may not have been familiar with TTT operations or with the functioning of parity groups as were some of the school and university representatives. There was also the possibility that some community representatives may not have had as much experience in participating in national conferences as had school and university people.

For this reason, on the afternoon prior to the first general session that evening there was an orientation program for community participants which was conducted by Mr. Anthony C. Gibbs (TTT LTI), Miss Marina Mercado (Northeast Cluster), Dr. Madelon D. Stent (Conference Co-Chairman), and Mr. Rudolph Salmeron (Midwest Cluster). While community representatives were specifically invited to attend this session, it was open to all participants. This session undoubtedly contributed to the effective part that community representatives played in the groups they joined.

The materials prepared for distribution at the Orientation Program for

OE: Office of Education in the Department of Health, Education, and Welfare (also referred to familiarly as HEW).

BEPD: Bureau of Educational Personnel Development.

TTT: Training the Teacher Trainers (funded by BEPD in HEW's OE).

TTT Clusters: Regional groupings of TTT projects that were established to facilitate communication among the projects.

TTT LTI: The Leadership Training Institute of TTT projects (a national advisory panel with representation from the community, the schools, and the universities).

Community Participants asked such questions as "What is TTT? What is the TTT purpose? What is parity in TTT projects? What does parity mean for the community members in the program or on the Advisory Council? Why should the community participants be concerned about 'thrust for action' coming out of this Conference on Cultural Pluralism? What role should we as community participants play at this conference?"

In order to make certain that the presenters, chairmen, and reactors would help focus the discussion on recommendations for action, there was also an orientation meeting for them on the same afternoon prior to the opening evening session. This meeting was conducted by Dr. Harry N. Rivlin (TTT LTI), Dr. Mary Jane Smalley (BEPD), Mrs. Raquel Montenegro (Conference Planning Committee), and Mrs. Margaret G. Labat (TTT LTI), and stressed both the general procedure for the conference and the ways in which the leadership teams and the other conference participants could focus attention on getting recommendation for action.

During the first general session, which was chaired by Dr. Madelon D. Stent, Conference Co-Chairman, the talk by Dr. Don Davies, then Associate Commissioner for Educational Personnel Development, was important not only for what he said in support of cultural pluralism but also because his very presence at the meeting, despite budgetary conferences going on in Washington at that moment, symbolized the importance that OE leaders attached to the conference. In order to afford every participant an overview of the entire program, each of the eight presenters gave a short account of his major thrust for action.

There were three sessions for each discussion group. For the first and third sessions, participants were assigned to specific groups in order to assure representation from each of the four sectors involved in TTT. The second session was a free choice one so that participants could go to the one that concerned them most. The charge to all groups was the same: Come up with the recommendations for action that will be most likely to advance cultural pluralism in education and in teacher education.

Three other activities were available to participants at times that did not conflict with either group sessions or general meetings. There was a Book Fair with an exhibit of books and other learning materials related to cultural pluralism. The Northeast Cluster had showings of films that are useful for teaching cultural pluralism. There was also a choice of five visits to places in the Chicago area that were deeply involved in cultural pluralism.

The convention concluded with a luncheon session, presided over by

Dr. William R. Hazard, Conference Co-Chairman, with Mr. Vine Deloria, Jr. speaking on the American Indian's approach to cultural pluralism.

How It All Began

Because the TTT projects are actively involved in implementing the concept that the education of teachers must involve the community, the liberal arts faculty, the school system, and the teacher education faculty on a parity basis, it was only natural that their activities should lead to the Conference on Education and Teacher Education for Cultural Pluralism. Similarly, because the TTT LTI had a major responsibility for seeing that the various TTT projects became part of a national thrust for significant change in education, it was again only natural that TTT LTI should now take as its major goal the task of seeing that the results of the conference should lead to change in education. Even so, the conference was more than the inevitable result of doing what comes naturally.

"The Year of the Liberal Arts" was the title given to an invitational conference for TTT program personnel which was conducted in Phoenix, Arizona, April 30-May 2, 1970. The report of that conference is entitled *The Liberal Arts and Teacher Education—A Confrontation*[2] but the highly charged confrontation that occurred on the last day of that conference was not part of the original plan.

"During the morning panel discussion session, Mr. Moses C. Davis arose to read . . . [a] position paper, which had been drawn up by twenty-seven members[3] of minority groups present at the conference, representatives, in

[2] Donald N. Bigelow, ed., *The Liberal Arts and Teacher Education—A Confrontation* (Lincoln, Neb.: University of Nebraska Press, 1971).

[3] The signers of this paper were: Claude Adams, Jacksonville, Tex.; William Brown, Hartford, Conn.; Edgar Burnett, St. Louis, Mo.; Jose Burruel, Phoenix, Ariz.; Henry Casso, Los Angeles, Cal.; Sara Collier, Denver, Colo.; Moses C. Davis, Wheat Ridge, Colo.; Maurice Eastmond, Brooklyn, N.Y.; Anthony C. Gibbs, Chicago, Ill.; Nancie L. Gonzalez, Iowa City, Iowa; Audrey Johnson, New York, N.Y.; Marie Johnson, Carbondale, Ill.; Theodore J. Johnson, Omaha, Neb.; J. B. Jones, Houston, Tex.; Louisa Lewis, Berkeley, Cal.; Frank Perry Jr., Lorman, Miss.; E. C. Powell, Hawkins, Tex.; Samuel Proctor, New Brunswick, N. J.; Earl Rand, Houston, Tex.; Ruby Riney, No. Minneapolis, Minn.; Madelon D. Stent, New York, N.Y.; Robert J. Terry, Houston, Tex.; Edgar R. Thomas, Columbus, Mo.; Ifekandu Umunna, Bloomfield, Conn.; Charles Z. Wilson, Pacific Palisades, Cal.; Amanda Williams, Berkeley, Cal.; Vivian Windley, New York, N.Y.

the main, of the black community, though some Chicano people were also included in the writing of the report."[4] Mr. Davis presented two motions, one of which was summarized by Dr. Donald Bigelow, Director, Division of College Programs, Bureau of Educational Personnel Development in the U.S. Office of Education, who was presiding, as "that the LTI(TTT) organize another conference, which would seek to represent the interests of those minority people not here adequately represented."[5] The motion was passed.

Fortunately, the legalistic technicalities which could have proved to be an obstacle to organizing a second conference had no such power. Since TTT LTI had no part in planning or conducting the Phoenix conference (the badge worn by the director of TTT LTI who did attend all but the last session clearly labeled him as "guest"), it did not have to accept a motion passed by that group. Instead of resorting to legalisms, however, the director of TTT LTI invited representative signers of the Phoenix protest to a meeting so that they could indicate the kind of conference they had in mind.

At a meeting held on October 19-20, 1970, TTT LTI agreed to sponsor a conference and to shoulder the major share of the costs involved. The Midwest TTT Cluster and the Northeast TTT Cluster agreed to co-sponsor the conference and to pay a lesser share of the costs. A planning committee was organized and in keeping with the· pattern of parity that prevails throughout the TTT Program, it consisted of community people, school personnel, and university faculty. Seeking to be representative in another sense, too, it had some members designated by the Black and Chicano signers of the Phoenix protest, members of TTT LTI, the Northeast and Midwest Cluster leaders who were co-sponsors of the conference, and members of the minority ethnic groups who had not been prominent in the Phoenix conference, for example, the American Indians, Asian Americans, and Puerto Ricans.[6]

If any lesson is to be learned from the activities of the Conference Planning Committee, it is that the Boy Scout motto "Be Prepared" is as important for those planning a national conference as it is for a classroom

[4] Bigelow, op. cit., p. 159.

[5] Ibid., p. 162.

[6] The members of the conference planning committee were: Harry N. Rivlin, chairman, Rosa Estades, Richard Ford, Anthony C. Gibbs, William R. Hazard, Duane S. Knos, Margaret G. Labat, Raquel Montenegro, Madelon D. Stent, and William Whitehead. Staff members were: Dorothy M. Fraser and Adele F. Larschan.

teacher planning a unit of study for pupils. Much of the success of the Conference on Education and Teacher Education for Cultural Pluralism must be attributed to the care with which the Conference Planning Committee attended to not only the major questions but also the many, many details that often mark the difference between an effective conference and chaos. For example, it had to make certain that using the Sheraton Blackstone Hotel in Chicago as the convention site would not offend the sensitivity of any ethnic group.

Three general principles were accepted from the very beginning. First, the conference was to lead to action rather than to only a published record of the papers presented. Second, in keeping with TTT emphasis on parity, the conference would involve participants from the community, the schools, and the universities. Third, members of various ethnic groups that had little part in the Phoenix conference would have a far greater role in the one on cultural pluralism and would have key roles as presenters of papers, discussion leaders, and reactors. It is comforting to be able to report that all of these principles were actually followed in practice at every stage of the conference.

Follow-Up

How successful the Conference on Education and Teacher Education for Cultural Pluralism would prove to be could not be determined as participants said "good-bye" to each other, while waiters cleared the tables, and technicians packed away their public-address microphones and speakers. An indication of the enthusiasm generated by the conference and of the general determination of the participants that the conference should be only the beginning and not the end of the drive for cultural pluralism is seen in the spontaneous organization by the participants of two groups which hopefully would get to work after the conference ended. The National Coalition for Cultural Pluralism sought to create a broad base for future action, with representation from many ethnic groups and from many occupations. The Temporary Steering Committee on Community Participation in Education hoped to prepare community members of TTT projects for a full realization of deferred dreams of equal access to educational opportunities.

Immediately below the last line of the conference program there appeared this note, which emphasized the determination of the Planning

Committee that the three-day meeting should not be an isolated event but rather a first step in implementing the concept of cultural pluralism in American schools:

For this conference to be productive, the recommendations which are formulated here must be translated into action. The group which sponsored this conference—TTT LTI, the Northeast TTT Cluster, and the Midwest TTT Cluster—will therefore plan appropriate follow-up activities.

These groups not only planned follow-up activities but began at once to carry them out. Within two weeks, the Conference Planning Committee met to examine and to act on the recommendations that had been submitted. Within three weeks, TTT LTI, joined as it always is by the TTT Cluster Leaders, decided unanimously and enthusiastically to give first priority to efforts for making cultural pluralism in education and teacher education a reality. In succeeding months the follow-up work was continued in the various ways that are described in the next paragraphs.

As noted above, the sessions in Chicago were deliberately structured so as to encourage participants to develop suggestions for action in support of the concept of cultural pluralism. Altogether, more than a hundred recommendations were formulated by the eight discussion groups. Some were focused directly on aspects of cultural pluralism and on means of making it a central factor in education, while others dealt with related concerns that were important to participants in the various groups. As might be expected when eight groups were working independently on a selected theme, the total list of recommendations included some repetition and overlapping.

All of the recommendations were studied by a subcommittee of TTT LTI, which undertook the job of combining those which expressed common ideas. The result was a final list of sixty-seven recommendations, thirty-one of which dealt with various aspects of cultural pluralism,[7] while the rest were addressed to questions of basic policies for federally funded programs, or to the improvement of other aspects of American school and college programs. The following examples of the first category indicate the kinds of emphases that conference participants hope to see developed in future OE programs.

[7]For a complete list of the major recommendations dealing with cultural pluralism, see Appendix C, pp. 154-158.

Cultural pluralism should be recognized in the selection of personnel for decision-making bodies in all federal education programs, so that minority communities will have a policy role in such programs. This principle should be applied at all levels of a program, from top-level positions in the USOE to the personnel of individual projects, and at the state and local levels. Particular communities that are involved in a specific program should be represented in the decision-making bodies of that program. That is, no group should have the right to assume representation for another minority community in determining policy for the program.

Each project should maintain an active policy-making board in which there is parity among community, school, and university. This board should be provided with resources for monthly review of project operations, with immediate feedback and program modification based on the board's recommendations.

A pool of consultants on culturally pluralistic learning materials should be established, with its members drawn from the community, school, and higher education sectors of TTT. The services of these consultants should be available to TTT projects for the development of culturally pluralistic materials.

The recommendations concerning school and college programs that were developed dealt chiefly with curriculum matters and with the preparation of professional personnel for culturally pluralistic education.

The following examples illustrate the nature and range of concerns that were expressed.

All learning materials that are used in school instruction—audio-visual materials, periodicals, etc., as well as textbooks—should be accurately representative of ethnic minorities so as to implement the concept of cultural pluralism. A condition for any school district to receive federal funds of any kind should be that it will utilize only materials that meet this criterion. Publishing companies which produce materials that do not meet this criterion should be boycotted.

Standardized tests should be used only for purposes of instructional diagnosis and improvement of individual children, not as a basis for excluding children from normal educational experiences. In all such testing, the tester must speak the language of the child and the test(s) should be selected with consideration for the cultural setting in which the child has grown. The tests must be administered and interpreted in terms of the child's background.

The arts should be recognized and utilized as a fundamental tool for understanding and developing the concept of cultural pluralism.

Bilingualism should be recognized as an asset, not a liability, and school programs should be structured to enable bilingual students to capitalize on this asset. For example, curriculum experiences should be developed to maximize the advantages of a bilingual, bicultural background.

Bilingual, bicultural paraprofessionals recruited from the community should be recognized as essential components of improved education for bilingual, bicultural children of the various ethnic groups; consequently universities and school districts should cooperate to provide adequate training programs for such community people.

The USOE, state education departments, and/or other educational agencies should develop a screening process that local schools can apply to determine that teachers, administrators, and other educational personnel who are newly employed, or who are to receive tenure, salary increment, or other advancement, have the understanding of cultural pluralism, the sensitivity, and the commitment required to implement improved education for children of all ethnic groups.

University programs for the preparation of teachers should be structured so as to provide both students and faculty with extensive experiences in the schools and in the organizations and agencies of the communities that are served by the schools. To insure integration of the field experiences into all parts of the program, faculty members who are not involved directly in these experiences should engage in in-service observations, seminars, and workshops focused on the schools and their communities. The various cultural groups in these communities should help to plan and implement the orientation of students and faculty to their particular cultures. To facilitate both the input from the community and the integration of the field experiences into more theoretical aspects of the teacher training program, many activities that traditionally have been conducted on campus should take place in school and community settings. One way of implementing this goal would be to have university faculty members given dual appointments in the university and the local school.

The USOE and other appropriate agencies should establish programs for the preparation of university faculty and for research in the various fields of ethnic studies, including research on the cognitive structures of minority cultures. Ethnic colleges should be established where feasible and advisable for the training of experts in these fields. One dimension of such programs should be the development of international cultural exchange as appropriate to the particular field of focus, e.g., with Spanish-speaking countries in the case of ethnic studies focused on Puerto Rican and Mexican-American cultures or with Eastern European countries in the case of Slavic studies.

The TTT LTI committee also identified the persons, organizations, or agencies which would be in a position to act on the various suggestions and listed for each of the sixty-seven recommendations the specific place or places to which it should be forwarded. Each recommendation was then transmitted to the indicated agencies by the Director of TTT LTI, with an explanatory letter which offered the full cooperation of the TTT LTI in achieving wide discussion of the concept of cultural pluralism and possible action for its implementation in education and teacher education. The correspondence which has ensued between the Director of TTT LTI and a number of recipients of the conference recommendations suggests that, at the least, a dialogue concerning the concept of cultural pluralism has been stimulated in the educational community.

Given the overall orientation of the TTT Program, it is hardly surprising that many of the TTT projects which are in operation in various parts of the country included elements related to the concept of cultural pluralism prior to the Chicago conference. For example, field experiences and study programs to help teacher trainers and prospective teachers become acquainted with various ethnic communities and develop appreciation for their culture are built into many of the projects. Participation of community representatives in setting policy for the program and in actually conducting it is another feature of most TTT projects. Emphasis on recruiting and training members of minority cultural groups as teachers, administrators, and teacher trainers is a third element that is found in many of the TTT projects. The development of curriculum materials and classroom activities that have relevance for particular groups, such as Chicano or American Indian children, has been undertaken in some projects.

Reports from the projects to the TTT program manager in the Office of Education suggest that these and other efforts related to the concept of cultural pluralism are being intensified during the current year, reflecting the experiences of the project representatives as participants in the conference. Thus the conference has reinforced and expanded efforts to implement cultural pluralism that has already been initiated.

In addition, special workshops and meetings have been held by several of the projects to provide for wider consideration of ideas relative to cultural pluralism that were presented in the various conference papers and in the discussion groups. In at least one case, these discussions were taped for future use in classes in the teacher education program.

The publication of this volume constitutes another aspect of the conference follow-up. Numerous requests for copies of the conference papers indicated a need for making available to a wide audience the range of ideas and proposals that were put forward by the various authors. Therefore, the conference papers appear as Chapters 3, 4, 6, 7, 8, 9, 10, 11, and 13, of this book. Two additional papers, one presenting the views of an Asian American and the other describing the implementation of cultural pluralism in an American Indian school, were solicited by the editors in order to round out the volume. The editors believe that these papers, with their varied approaches to the question of cultural pluralism in education, will stimulate thought, discussion, and action. The views expressed in these chapters are, of course, those of the individual authors rather than statements of policy that have been endorsed by the sponsors of the conference or the editors of this volume.

During the months since the conference, TTT LTI has organized itself into subcommittees to plan for a variety of activities that will support the concept of cultural pluralism in education and teacher education. Some of these, such as the preparation of collections of carefully selected materials dealing with various cultural groups or the sponsoring of small working conferences for specific personnel, are relatively short range and can be carried through in the near future. Others look ahead to the time when the TTT Program (and TTT LTI) will no longer be in existence as an entity and seek to provide continuing mechanisms for making the concept of cultural pluralism a central factor in American schools and in the preparation of teachers for these schools.

At this writing, TTT LTI is in the process of establishing priorities among the several activities which its subcommittees have proposed and of determining and establishing a time schedule for those that are finally decided upon. While it is too early to cite specifics in this conference report, it is clear that substantial efforts for developing and implementing the concept of cultural pluralism in education and teacher education are under way.

While TTT LTI can assume the leadership in this thrust for cultural pluralism, it will need active cooperation and support from the Office of Education, from the TTT Projects and Clusters, from the communities, from the schools and universities, and from all professional and civic organizations who share these aspirations. Steps to mobilize this support have already been taken and much more needs to be done—but that is another story that can be told only long after the Conference on Education and Teacher Education for Cultural Pluralism has been concluded.

2

CULTURAL PLURALISM AND SCHOOLING:
SOME PRELIMINARY OBSERVATIONS

WILLIAM R. HAZARD AND MADELON D. STENT

Today, education is perhaps the most important function of state and local governments .... In these days, it is doubtful that any child may reasonably be expected to succeed in life if he is denied the opportunity of an education. Such an opportunity, where the state has undertaken to provide it, is *a right which must be made available to all on equal terms.* [emphasis added] .

U. S. Supreme Court
Brown v. *Board of Education* (1954)

The melting-pot ideology has failed. Society is splintered and the youth of America desperately are seeking their identity. Cultural pluralism is both a fact and a concept which has not been given due recognition. The fact that the United States includes citizens of diverse cultures cannot be challenged. The extent to which the nonwhite cultures have been disenfranchised or made invisible varies but their existence is a fact. Treated as bare fact, cultural pluralism means very little. Moving from fact to concept, however, opens the door to useful examination. Once cultural pluralism is viewed conceptually as well as affectively, its implications for education and teacher education can be explored.

[13

Fortunately, the concept of cultural pluralism has not yet been carved in stone. There is still opportunity to discuss, debate, explore its dimensions, and to arrange its elements in more than one way. There are some once-useful concepts which, alas, by accident or design, have become frozen into forms that may have been functional in an earlier day but have only limited utility in the technological society of late twentieth century America. For example, the once-noble notion of democratic education now carries to those who are excluded threatening reminders of what it means in actual practice; not cultural freedom and action but cultural imperialism. The phrase "individual differences" continues to describe a basic truth about people but it cannot be used, as it sometimes is, to explain away inequitable educational opportunities. Whether or not cultural pluralism eventually goes to the conceptual graveyard depends, to a considerable extent, on our ability to translate the fact into effective action before its conceptual arteries harden.

A working definition, blending fact and concept, developed out of discussions of the National Coalition for Cultural Pluralism. This group, formed at the Conference on Education and Teacher Education for Cultural Pluralism, defined cultural pluralism as

a state of equal co-existence in a mutually supportive relationship within the boundaries or framework of one nation of people of diverse cultures with significantly different patterns of belief, behavior, color, and in many cases with different languages. To achieve cultural pluralism, there must be unity with diversity. Each person must be aware of and secure in his own identity, and be willing to extend to others the same respect and rights that he expects to enjoy himself.

A statement outlining the National Coalition's position on cultural pluralism is included in Appendix A, pp. 149-150. This definition provides an operational framework for implementing the conference recommendations, which appear in Appendix C, pp. 154-158.

Little need be added to the definition but some interpretation is in order. One might quarrel with "equal coexistence"; it hardly carries the feeling of people living and working toward human goals. There is a connotation of grudging admission of another's right of being, feeling, and aspiring. Further, there appears to be undue narrowness in limiting the mutually supportive relationships to people of "one nation." Surely, one could argue that cultural pluralism is a human condition, international in scope, and transcending national boundaries. Rather than quibble over this definition, however, a more useful reaction might be to extend, expand, and develop it.

The concept of cultural pluralism must include basic ideas of equal opportunity for all people, respect for human dignity, and the power to control the significant environmental and psychological forces impinging on people. "Mutually supportive relations" must not be confused with tolerance. To confuse tolerance and "mutually supportive relationships" is patronizing. Toleration of another person diminishes that individual, while mutual support enhances all who participate in the common effort. To regard human dignity as a grant bestowed by "me" on "you" or by "you" on "me" is to miss the point completely. Despite a bloody world history of cultural exploitation, cultures have rights paralleling those of people. Recognition of the "other" culture must not depend on a gesture by a people or a government: after all, we give no prizes for recognizing that the sun rises or the dew falls. Culture is the core of man's being: what he was, is, and ought to be. It simply is a fact.

To accept the concept of cultural pluralism is likewise no cause for fanfare. For too long we have tended to treat the performance of human duties and the recognition of human rights as acts of charity. We have every obligation to accept cultures different from our own. The familiar game of granting national "days" or "weeks" to human relations is rather silly when you ponder it. The late Philip Wylie once noted that the child's first lesson in graft occurs when we give him a gold star for doing what he should do anyway. Perhaps we grown-ups have confused our means and ends in similar fashion. In any event, cultural pluralism simply "is." The failure of individuals or groups to understand this reality complicates the problem rather than denies the existence of the concept. Cultural pluralism includes recognition, acceptance, and support of all cultures. It includes gut-level respect for human dignity and human differences. Perhaps it carries the simplistic figure of the golden rule with teeth.

The insistence that education address itself to cultural diversity motivated the national Conference on Education and Teacher Education for Cultural Pluralism. At this unique and multi-ethnic gathering, the validity of the concept of cultural pluralism as opposed to racism, and its ramifications for teacher education were at last opened up and catalogued. The definition of the concept and its potential as a philosophical base for building guidelines for teacher education was spearheaded by representatives selected by culturally pluralistic groups across this country. Teacher education, with the support of the United States Office of Education, was at last taking the giant and humanistic step of asking those consumers of education what should be priorities in the training of teachers. By organizing a conference around understanding man's unique cultural diversity, a new sense of the beauty of a common humanity was created.

The common concern of the conference was education and the parallel concerns were the several aspects of cultural pluralism. Each participant had a vested interest inasmuch as all people have a stake in human problems. The concept of cultural pluralism is especially appropriate for government-funded projects. In essence, that's what many are all about. Schools, teachers, and teacher training are the logical vehicles to develop the attitudes, understandings, and action necessary to implement the concept.

This book examines racial tensions and conflict as a major educational problem within the historical perspective of educators' and community leaders' efforts to cope with institutional racism. From the conference standpoint, integration is no longer the relevant issue. The focus on techniques for achieving peaceful and orderly change has been modified by the nonwhite community's strategic digression from integration. In large measure, the drive toward integration has been overshadowed by demands for group identity, somewhere on the continuum between separation and community self-determination. To function effectively in a pluralistic relationship, each group needs to define its own cultural base and develop a pervasive sense of cultural identity, as well as cultural unity. In order to accomplish this cultural unity, the racial and ethnic groups separate prior to negotiating back into pluralism. After separation, subsequent negotiations with others may proceed from genuine strength rather than traditional stereotyped cultural positions.

Social justice as a treasured American concept may then take on real meaning in practice, as each group may define and demand equality of opportunity and constitutional protection. Cultural pluralism as a philosophy and strategy is all-encompassing and means coexistence of these separated, and significantly distinct groups.

Cultural pluralism is not an assimilative posture; it is a negation of assimilation. It is a posture which maintains that there is more than one legitimate way of being human without paying the penalties of second-class citizenship, and that this pluralism would enrich and strengthen the nation. Social justice, alone, means a fair share of the pie; as a goal in the United States it has usually meant an assimilative attitude. Cultural pluralism, on the other hand, calls unavoidably for a pluralistic viewpoint; it demands the same fair share *plus the right not to assimilate.*[1]

The nineteenth century "melting-pot" mythology of cultural sameness is no longer accepted by substantial segments of either minority cultures or of the dominant group. The familiar cycle of racial crises leading from conquest, exploitation, slavery, segregation, and discrimination to ghettos, reservations, and poverty, with regular stops along the way for frustration and rage, is not acceptable. Our national social alternatives are not limited to the melting-pot assimilation or separatism. Some workable expression of cultural pluralism is clearly a third and, to many people, the only viable alternative.

The determination by Chicanos, Puerto Ricans, Asian Americans, American Indians, and Blacks to reject integration is based on their experience in America. This experience includes the snail-paced desegregation of public schools and universities, the incredible scarcity of Indian, Chicano, and other nonwhite scholars among the brain sculptors of society, and our peculiarly egotistical policy of defining and solving world issues from the white man's perspective. In the classrooms of this country, integration has too often assumed that nonwhite students must be inculcated with the prevailing white values before they can be truly "educated" in the transmitted tradition of American culture.

In similar fashion, teacher education programs perpetuate the notion that middle-class white "standards" and middle-class white "excellence" are the ultimate tests of legitimacy and approval. Culturally pluralistic education flatly rejects this notion. Rather, it demands standards drawn from more than one culture. Characteristics of excellence must not be restricted to the dominant white culture. We rarely ask professional educators to examine the bases of their judgment of standards. The stress on achievement tests for children and "measuring up to standards" in professional education has meant to teachers of minority group students measuring up to culturally biased "white" standards.

Some data on school populations may give needed perspective to the reality of cultural diversity. In the fall of 1970, over 51 million children were enrolled in public and private elementary and secondary schools. The most recent (1968) data indicate that 14.5 percent (6,282,200) pupils

[1] Unpublished paper prepared by Bruce Gaarder, United States Office of Education, 1971.

were Black, 4.6 percent (2,003,000) were Spanish Americans, and 142,630 (less than .05 percent) were American Indians.[2] Predictably, the twenty-one largest school systems reported substantially different racial-cultural "mixes" in their school districts for the same year (1968).[3] Of the total pupil population of 4,728,886, Black pupils numbered 1,921,465 (40.6 percent); 502,598 (10.6 percent) were Spanish American; 7,912 (0.2 percent) were American Indians; and 68,680 (1.5 percent) were Oriental. The remainder of 4,228,231 (47.1 percent), including Caucasian, were reported as "others."

Taking Chicago as an example, the most recent published enrollment figures for the city's public schools reveal the ethnic and racial distribution for 1970 and 1971:[4]

	1970		1971	
	Number	%	Number	%
Caucasian	199,969	34.6	188,312	32.8
Black	316,711	54.8	320,797	55.8
American Indian	1,042	.2	1,184	.2
Oriental	3,883	.7	4,424	.8
Latin	56,374	9.7	59,778	10.4
(Mexican)	(24,066)	(4.2)	(25,314)	(4.4)
(Puerto Rican)	(26,176)	(4.5)	(27,303)	(4.8)
(Cuban)	(2,673)	(.4)	(3,510)	(.6)
(Other Latin)	(3,459)	(.6)	(3,351)	(.6)
Total	577,679	100.0	574,495	100.0

Obviously, in most of the largest urban centers, the so-called cultural and ethnic minorities constitute a majority. To postulate our education on bases other than cultural diversity and pluralistic notions seems to ignore the realities of our schools' population.

The retreat from integration, as it has been practiced, does not necessarily mean permanent separation. Substantial segments of excluded ethnic cultures no longer accept either the culture or proclaimed wisdom of white America when to do so violates the integrity of the minority cultures. For

---

[2] U.S. Department of Commerce, Statistical Abstract of the United States, 1971.

[3] Atlanta, Baltimore, Boston, Buffalo, Chicago, Cleveland, Dallas, Denver, Detroit, Los Angeles, Memphis, Milwaukee, Minneapolis, New York, Philadelphia, Pittsburgh, Portland, St. Louis, San Diego, San Francisco, and Washington, D.C.

[4] *Chicago Tribune,* November 23, 1971, sec. 3, p. 14.

minority cultures, a new strategy for teacher education can come about only if the educational and economic-political world system, as the white man has constructed it, is demystified, analyzed, and revealed for what it is in actual operation. Much of what is commonly labeled history is more like a fable—a distorted fable at that. Carter Woodson, a Black scholar, noted in 1937:

In our own particular history we should not dim one bit the luster of any star in our firmament. Let no one be so thoughtless as to decry the record of the makers of the United States of America. We should not learn less of George Washington, "First in War, First in Peace, and First in the hearts of his countrymen"; but we should learn something also of the three thousand Negro soldiers of the American revolution who helped to make this "Father of our Country" possible .... We should in no way whatever withhold assistance from the effort to make the world safe for democracy, but we should teach our citizenry history rather than propaganda and thus make this country safe for all elements of the population at home.[5]

In this context, cultural pluralism clearly requires that due recognition be given to all contributions to our national heritage. This heritage, when correctly written, will include the contributions of Blacks, Browns, Reds, Yellows, as well as Whites. There will be no need to suppress the contributions and heroes of some cultures; honest reporting of facts will be adequate to substantially rewrite our history. American history, after all, began long before Plymouth Rock felt the first step of the Pilgrims. There will be no need for patronizing put-downs and exclusion by historians; honest assessments of the excluded ethnic participation by minority scholars will result in a rather different national story.

Schools, universities, and teacher-training institutions will have to do more than add courses to the curriculum. Space limitations do not permit more than a surface view of the implications of cultural pluralism to teacher education, but a few more comments are needed. Ethnic minority "studies" certainly open doors to the rediscovery of pride in self and cultural values. To believe, as some do, that these studies stop there is to negate their validity as a highly intellectual venture. A "true" ethnic studies program would never leave unexamined the dominant, pervasive cultural assumptions underlying both schooling and teacher training. Education that recognizes the fact of cultural pluralism must raise new

[5] Carter G. Woodson, "The Story of the Negro Retold," (*Journal of the Association for the Study of Negro Life and History*, 1935).

empirical questions about the cultural values of our society. It must challenge the assumption that bilingualism and biculturalism are handicaps; we may well discover them to be distinct advantages. It must challenge the economic and political systems which predictably and systematically oppress Blacks, Chicanos, Asian Americans, American Indians, the poor and those so patronizingly labeled "disadvantaged." Such education will explore the problems of governance, taxation, welfare, voting, and quality of schooling, as well as the total range of national priorities. Most importantly, it will challenge young minds to ask pertinent questions and to seek viable solutions.

One direction for cultural pluralism in education challenges our minds. The evidence clearly shows that America is a pluralistic rather than an integrated society. The only real possibility for equality, then, is through group or ethnic parity. Some religious, ethnic, and racial groups have achieved parity; the Chicanos, Puerto Ricans, Blacks, American Indians, and other nonwhites have not even achieved the facade of equality, but have been kept on the fringe of society. Ours is a deeply racist, hypocritical society which professes belief in equality for all, yet provides equality for selected citizens, often at the expense of those who are culturally and linguistically different. These excluded groups have begun to relate to each other in order to preserve each one's own culture, tradition, and sense of community. The path toward cultural pluralism allows for being both equal and separate.

The implications of cultural pluralism for education and teacher education are monumental. For schools and universities to accept cultural pluralism as both fact and concept would revolutionize what passes now for schooling and teacher training. The basic assumptions underlying school governance, curriculum, academic and nonacademic standards, and educational reward systems would be dramatically reformed. The school mission, now focused on conformity to monolithic social and intellectual expectations, necessarily would broaden and, paradoxically, would narrow on a new focus. At the present time schools (and teacher-producing institutions for that matter) struggle to build defensible rationales for failure. Elaborate justifications emerge to explain why substantial numbers of children do not learn and substantial numbers of teachers cannot teach. For those students who come from cultural settings deviant from the assumed "norm," schooling constitutes a threatening low-win or no-win experience. Their cultural "differences" are treated as handicaps, as burdens, and as shortcomings to be overcome. The identification of poor and culturally different children is the first step in the program of rejection. In essence, our schooling machinery advises these children to "shape up (i.e., drop those differences, and fast) or ship out." Alan Exelrod, analyzing the impact of the *Swann*[6] decision on Chicano education, pointed to the tragic price of ignoring minority cultures.

The Chicano child brings to the school a different culture and language than that of the Anglo. When he comes to the school he is often forbidden to speak his native language and his cultural traditions are ignored. Often the school he attends is inferior to the school just down the road attended primarily by Anglos. He sees few Chicano teachers and fewer Chicano administrators. His academic life is tainted with the prejudice and the indifference of Anglo teachers who see little prospect for his academic success. He sees his brothers and sisters shunted into the mentally retarded classes even though these same siblings care for the whole family when the parents are working. The end result is alienation from school, and eventual dropping out. . . . the high dropout rate reflects the psychological damage done to the child by the school.[7]

In this regard let us look at the educational issues in the *Diana* case,[8] which could easily become substantive content within a teacher education course of study. The Education Code of California, as in many other states, maintains separate specialized classes for mentally retarded children. Educators and others recognize that, because of the inherent stigma in such classification, great injustice would be done should a child be incorrectly placed.

In California, between the ages of four and eight, a number of school children are given either the Stanford-Binet or Wexler (WISC) only in English to measure their intelligence ability. A score of 70-55 on the WISC test or 68-52 on the Stanford-Binet results in the child being placed in an EMR (Educable Mentally Retarded) class. In this test case the children were nine Mexican-American children and had been placed in an EMR class. When tested solely in English by a non-Spanish speaking tester, the scores ranged from 30-70 with a mean score of 63½. On November 1 and 2, 1969, each was individually retested on WISC test (in English and/or

[6] *Swann* v. *Charlotte-Mecklenburg Board of Education, et al.,* 91 S.Ct. 1267 (1971).

[7] Alan Exelrod, "Chicano Education: In *Swann's* Way?," *Inequality in Education*, no. 9 (August 3, 1971) p. 31.

[8] *Diana et al.* v. *State Board of Education,* U.S. District Court, Northern District of California No. C-7037 RFP.

Spanish) and each was permitted to respond in either language. Seven of the nine had a score ranging from 2 to 19 points over the maximum for mentally retarded with an average of 8½ points over the cut-off. One of the other two scored right on the line, and the ninth student was three points below.

Diana's score improved 49 ponts over an earlier Stanford-Binet test. Her brother's score jumped 22 points; three other children showed gains of 20, 14, and 10 points with the average gain being 15 points.

In California there are approximately 85,000 children in EMR classes. A study of the racial distribution in the state's public schools during the 1966-67 school year revealed that 26% of the children in EMR classes were of Spanish surname, while such students comprised only 13% of the total student population. It is statistically impossible that this maldistribution occurred by random chance (odds in excess of 1 in 100 billion).

In June of 1969, John Plakos of the California Department of Education randomly selected 47 Mexican-American children in EMR classes within the State. Fifty percent were in urban areas and 50% were rural, and they were retested in Spanish. Forty-two of the 47 scored over the IQ ceiling for MR classification; 37 scored 75 or higher; over half scored higher than 80 and one sixth of them scored in the 90's or 100's. Their average improvement over earlier tests was 13.15 IQ points. . . . both sides to the action signed a stipulation and a consent decree was signed. . . . The main points of the Court Order and agreement were that all children whose primary home language is other than English (e.g., Spanish, Chinese, etc.) must be tested in both their primary language and in English. They may be tested only with tests or sections of tests that do not depend on such things as vocabulary, general information (who wrote *Romeo and Juliet?*) and other similar unfair verbal questions.

The State psychologists are to work on normalizing a new or revised IQ test to reflect Mexican-American culture. This test will be normalized by giving it only to California Mexican-Americans so that in the future Mexican-American children tested will be judged only by how they compare to the performance of their peers, not the population as a whole. And finally, any school district which has a significant disparity between the percentages of Mexican-American students in its regular classes and in its classes for the retarded must submit an explanation setting out the reasons for their disparity.[9]

The study of cases such as this, within the context of cultural pluralism,

[9] Charles D. and Rita M. Boags, "The Misuse of a So-Called Psychological Examination for the Selection of Jurors" in Charles W. Thomas, *Boys No More: A Black Psychologists View of Community* (Beverly Hills, Calif.: Glencoe Press, 1971). Reprinted by permission of the author and the Glencoe Press.

would do much to reshape teacher education. The curriculum, that is the "content," would be derived from the living cultures and problems of our pluralistic society. The learnings or perceptions for the student would be a humanistic and cognitive experience in understanding the technological racism in some scientific testing, as well as its resultant loss of human productivity. Each child brings a valuable life experience, a heritage, if you prefer, to the school experience. Who decided that unitary goals were required for all children? Are uniform standards, goals, and expectations expressions of superior virtues or are they expressions of inferior imagination? Such questions, when raised by ghetto parents to educators, generally unleash clouds of jargonized "professional" replies. The educators' retreat to "professional" responses clouds issues rather than clears the air. One educator, perhaps uncommonly candid, put the matter this way:

Frantically trying to establish professionalism and prevent parental interference, educators have let loose a smoke screen of scientific jargon which obscures rather than clarifies issues. Only in the past decade, thanks to the civil rights and black movements, has the smoke screen lifted to reveal schoolmen trying to cover up their professional nakedness by blaming parents for low reading and achievement scores. Thus "professionalism" has been a code word for keeping parents at arms length, for resisting the development of any meaningful face-to-face contact between school and parent, between teacher and community. Because schoolmen react negatively to inquiries about performance of youngsters, teachers, or the school, no personal relationships with the broad spectrum of the community can materialize.[10]

The assumptions underlying behavioral and performance "standards" are hateful and destructive to those unfortunates inevitably in the left-hand side of the bell-shaped social curve. David Selden, national president of the American Federation of Teachers, in testimony to the Senate Select Committee on Equal Educational Opportunity, noted:

If we accept graduation from high school as the minimum definition of what constitutes "an education," American schools, even by their own standards, educate only half the children of the nation. Half of those who enter 1st grade never make it through the 12th grade. Somewhere along the line they become dropouts, fallouts, or pushouts.[11]

[10] Larry Cuban, "Teacher and Community," *Harvard Educational Review* XXXIX, 2 (Spring, 1969).

[11] *Chicago Tribune*, October 15, 1971, sec. 1, p. 24.

The price we pay for cultural singularism is unduly high; human economics alone argues most eloquently for cultural pluralism. By broadening the assumption base from monolithic sameness to cultural pluralism, education and teacher education could sharpen and focus their currently fuzzy and overboard objectives. If individual differences among children (and teachers) mean anything at all, surely it means respect for and, so far as possible, support of their cultural differences. The great bulk of school curriculum material is based on the cultural melting-pot construct, through which singular (and artificial) cultural values are transmitted (and usually transmuted). The operating principle seems to be that all cultures, thereby, are equal with the dominant culture being more equal than the others. It is hardly surprising to note that few pupils or parents, other than those from the dominant cultures, are particularly satisfied with things curricular. If adult dissatisfaction and hassling were the only price, one might excuse our proceeding down such a wrong-headed path. The tragic and unrecompensable price, however, is the damage to relatively helpless and certainly innocent children. They are victimized twice: once by emerging from schooling with distorted (up or down) self-concepts and distorted cultural concepts; and twice over for those who are eased out of schooling through one or another of our systemic trapdoors. We repeat, the price is far too great.

Friendly and less-than-friendly critics may insist that even if the case for cultural pluralism is made, the transition from idea to action must yet be made. Further, it is one thing to propose a different life-view and another to live it. Such criticism (or, more properly, reaction) is both fair and expected. To understand and accept cultural pluralism as an operating concept for schooling is but a first step. Important, but still a first step. Beyond lies the awesome task of reshaping educational practices to achieve desired outcomes. The curricula need reform; teachers and administrators need training and retraining; parents and citizens will need to think through the implications of culture, schooling, and educational outcomes. In New York City, for example, two private schools have used the "Harlem Six" case[12] in projects studying the media and the criminal justice system. In one of the schools the case is being studied as an example of the treatment of minority groups by the criminal justice

---

[12]*People of the State of New York* v. *Baker et al.*, 23 N.Y. 2d 307 (1968). The Harlem Six were arrested in 1964 on charges of a Blood Brotherhood. Tried en masse in 1965, their guilty verdict was reversed in 1968 by the State Court of Appeals. Two are now undergoing retrial (1971).

system. Pupils will make reports on the court sessions they attend and publicize this information for their school paper. Such a focus for pupils as well as for teachers will prepare them for dealing with scholarly and socially significant topics that have not been adequately included in the social studies curriculum. Culturally pluralistic-based teacher education will have to deal also with the issue of the teachers' need for conceptual cultural enrichment and the "how" of translating this new content into learning for children.

Trite as it may sound, the nation, as a nation, will have to rethink its educational priorities. The level of difficulty anticipated in such educational reform should measure its importance rather than gauge its possibility. Cultural pluralism is a fact in our society; whether we do or do not adopt it as a working concept in education will not deny its existence.

Too many good ideas, including "creativity," "democracy," "individualized instruction," and "humanism" have drowned in a sea of friendly rhetoric. Perhaps this untimely death by popularity relates to the observation, attributed to James Farmer, that "ours (the Western) may be the only society to move from barbarism to decadence without passing through civilization."

America must rediscover itself. Cultural pluralism, with its ramifications for individual and ethnic truth, can lead us from the trap of racism and the destructive racial fictions on which our society has rested. This mandate cannot be realized by any single group; it requires each of the groups that make up America to tell and retell its own history and culture. Cultural pluralism permits parity among ethnic groups with differing powers and size. It can create a new way of life which rests on the right of all groups to maintain their cultural heritage. Cultural pluralism is a new direction for action in white and nonwhite relations, as the distinguished American educators and spokesmen so passionately expound in this report. Through culturally pluralistic education, we have a new basis for developing a richness of life in our society deriving from the unique strengths of each of its parts.

3

BILINGUAL AND BICULTURAL EDUCATION

MANUEL H. GUERRA

My paper explores two main areas: first, bilingual and bicultural education in a monolingual and monocultural frame of reference, and second, bilingual and bicultural education as a valuable intrinsic innovation of American curricula and a necessary extrinsic influence on basic American institutions. The first concerns the philosophical and pedagogical context in which bilingual and bicultural education reside in American schools and thought, and the second concerns an analysis of the merits of bilingual and bicultural education per se, its contribution to democratic thinking, and its effect upon the total curriculum.

It is the express purpose of this paper to elucidate the philosophical and historical background in which bilingual and bicultural education now functions and recommend to this conference specific ways in which bilingual and bicultural education may be understood, improved, and expanded.

Monolingual and monocultural education in America has traditionally ignored the cultural pluralism of American society. We acknowledge ethnic and racial differences, religious variances, and a cultural heterogeneity of our cities, but the criteria of our value judgments, our value system, and our social consciousness remain predominantly White Anglo-Saxon Protestant—that is, representative of the monolingual, monocultural predominant society. The dichotomy between this cultural pluralism of America on the one hand, and the imposing conformity of the monolingual and monocultural predominant society on the other, is something that has never been reconciled.

The melting-pot concept of acculturation and its inherent racism which was imposed upon American minorities, and which was unopposed in many responsible quarters of American society, only recently has been repudiated for its lack of social democracy and humanity. However, the same frame of mind which conceived this concept still dominates American education as well as the national image, and it is reinforced in our classrooms, in our textbooks, and in our mass media. This monolingual and monocultural attitude toward American society is a form of ethnocentrism which betrays our fundamental belief in the equality of man. It is an attack upon our basic American institutions and the fabric of our system of laws.

Indeed, the ambivalence between promises and practices of our historical declaration of human rights may be observed in our treatment of the American Indian and the Black man. This ambivalence may be found between our commitments to the Mexican government in the Articles of the Treaty of Guadalupe Hidalgo concerning the rights and privileges of the conquered Mexican people and the treatment of these people and their American descendants in the Southwestern United States. This ambivalence may be seen in the treaties and promises the United States government made to Indian tribes and the way both treaties and promises were broken. This dualism may be observed in the promises made to the Black man and the way Blacks have been treated in America.

Such contradictions started in the cradle of America when Lafayette, Pulaski, and Miranda, three American Revolutionary fathers, identified with the new cause, strengthened the position of George Washington, risked their lives and the lives of their men, despite the fact that none could speak English. Yet, how many textbooks tell you that none of the three was articulate in English? The point is germane to bilingualism because fluency in the English language was never a qualification for patriotic duty, but the barrier was subsequently raised for the privileges of citizenship when the Chicano was deprived voting rights at the polls because he could not speak English. Perhaps we should be reminded that the lack of ability to articulate in English has not kept our Chicanos from dying in Vietnam, for their casualties are three times their ratio to the population of the nation.

Indeed, there has been no reconciliation between the provincial and the international, between the universal and the chauvinistic, between the inclusive and the exclusive attitudes toward diversity of American societies and cultures. Ethnic and racial barriers separate our feeling and thinking, so much so that Americans have been taught to identify virtue and values in the idiom and terms of their own image, and not in the image of those with different color. While we dispossessed the Indian from his lands in the name of Manifest Destiny, we also read Thomas Paine's *The Rights of Man*, and the name of Monticello was as sacred to the nation as Jeffersonian Democracy itself. We sought unity in the Industrial Revolution, the expansion of the West, and the highest standard of living of any nation in the world. But we lost the fraternity that once brought us together, the reason for our sacrifices in the first place, and our faith in social justice and freedom.

This disparity between the ideal and the real in American life and the inequities between the disadvantaged and the affluent are the true context of bilingual and bicultural education today. In California, perhaps the nation's largest and wealthiest state, we find tragic examples of the predominance of monocultural attitudes in matters of history, law, and heritage. Spanish and Mexican explorers and statesmen are often ignored in our textbooks, classrooms, and communities. Portola, Vallejo, and Pablo de la Guerra do not receive the respect they merit, despite the fact that the latter was the author of the constitution of California written in Spanish. Governor Michelterena, founder of the public school system of California, is totally forgotten. For example, there is no public school named after him throughout the state.

In New Mexico, Juan de Oñate founded the state a generation before the Pilgrims landed on Plymouth Rock, but forty-two out of forty-nine popular textbooks omitted his name, while the men named George Oglethorp, William Penn, and Roger Williams were prominently described. Cabeza de Vaca, Fray Marcos de Niza, and the Black, Estebanico, who explored Arizona, are seldom mentioned in the saga of the West.

What is important is that these are not isolated examples, but illustrations of the monolingual and monocultural frame of reference that predominates in our schools, textbooks, and communities.

Spanish and Mexican laws, like the Spanish language, were practiced and used in Texas, Colorado, New Mexico, Arizona, and California. The Spanish language has antecedents and roots in this geographical area, just like French in Louisiana and Maine; German in Wisconsin; Swedish,

Norwegian, and Danish in Minnesota; Polish in Chicago and Detroit; Italian in Cleveland and Buffalo; Chinese in San Francisco; Japanese in Los Angeles; Portuguese in Rhode Island and California; Hebrew and Puerto Rican Spanish in New York City; etc.

It is noteworthy that the Spanish language was used in California courtrooms until the 1870s. The New Mexico unicameral legislature used Spanish until 1941. And in some areas of Southern Colorado, East Los Angeles, and El Paso, Texas, more Spanish may be heard than English. In New Mexico, where the Spanish-speaking citizens retained possession of their lands, became the body politic, and participated in public and civic policy-making affairs, bilingualism was an accepted government practice. However, when the majority of the Anglo citizens of New Mexico controlled the body politic, bilingualism was discontinued as state policy. This example illustrates how the monolingual and monocultural American seeks conformity of others to the ways of his own culture, and entertains little respect for the heritage of his fellow citizens.

There is something unique about the American Indian and the Mexican American in terms of cultural pluralism, national identity, and citizenship. Both were indigenous to the land before the coming of the Anglo-Saxon; both were conquered by military intervention and action; both owe their existence to treaties and pacts between military governors, chiefs, and heads of state; both were forced to accept conditions of war and peace, upon which future relationships were predicated, in contrast to European immigrants who came to America fleeing persecution, famine, and unemployment, many of whom were anxious to change their identity and adopt an Anglo lifestyle. The American Indian and Mexican American both had a rich heritage: neither wanted to surrender it. And both resisted the imposition of the Anglo lifestyle as a condition of citizenship, employment, or education. Indeed, the dropout rate of the Mexican American child, the highest in the nation, does not only prove the obsolescence and failure of school systems, but also the tragic alienation of the bilingual in a monolingual society and the defensive pride that resists repression. This inherent lack of respect by the dominant society for the human element is at the bottom of the problem. Both Indians and Mexicans lost the war; they lost their lands, their political rights, and their social status. However, both struggle today to preserve their cultural identity. Until very recently, the monolingual and monocultural approach to the problems of the Indian, Chicano, and Puerto Rican at most have been good intentions with bad results, and more often a rude imposition of undemocratic concepts and practices. Lack of motivation, lack of relevancy to instruction, high dropout rates, and indifference—how else can the human being show displeasure toward education that oppresses personal dignity and self expression?

Cultural pluralism in education is recognition of the facts and the truth about people and society in America. It encompasses *all* people of the United States, their racial and ethnic differences, their customs and traditions, their language and religious preferences. Cultural pluralism is keenly aware of and deeply respects cultural differences in America, and subscribes to the view that this diversity contributes strength, variety, and beauty to all walks of American life. It is precisely this view of America that has not predominated in our classrooms, textbooks, and mass media.

The values of bilingual and bicultural education today may be accountable in the following manner:

1. Serious educational inequities of the disadvantaged, handicapped and poor are being corrected. Children with language barriers who need special teachers and teacher aids, textbooks and materials geared to their needs, and the teacher-pupil rapport which builds confidence, a feeling of adequacy, and a better self-image, are receiving these for the first time.

2. The use of the domestic language in the classroom in both Title VII and Title I programs, for example, helps the child acquire basic skills and knowledge in subjects such as mathematics rather than wait for the child to achieve language proficiency before exposing him to new learning. Before, the child waited to develop proficiency in the English language, and in the process, became retarded among his peer group. English is taught concurrently with the domestic language, and faster and more effective learning of English results whenever the domestic language is considered an asset rather than a liability. Educational goals endeavor to supplement rather than substitute the domestic language, and the latter is viewed not only in the best interests of the child for purposes of enrichment, but also in the best interests of society and the nation.

3. The encouragement and maintenance of second and third languages is considered a vast reservoir of American talent. This concept, which is not entertained by monolingual and monocultural Americans, nevertheless is officially recognized as a valuable asset and talent. American public schools should do all they can to preserve second language talents on the part of children. Second language instruction should be encouraged and developed in the elementary schools whenever possible, and language instruction in schools with large bilingual attendance should be re-evaluated and overhauled. Second language instruction in junior high school and

senior high school should be geared to the social needs of the nation and not to the fairy tales and folklore of exotic places. We have concerned ourselves too much with castles in Spain, Gauchos in Argentina, and the pronunciation of the Castilian lisp, and we have ignored Joe Garcia and his family who live next door.

For the first time in America, second languages are being sponsored for immediate social purpose and not for long-range goals and future promises. Bilingualism and biculturalism have to do with the improvement of the lives of Americans and their struggle for survival, and the coexistence of American societies in workable and trustworthy relationships. Bilingualism is not an elective, not a college-bound program, not a romantic interlude to faraway places, but a realistic approach to the needs and suffering of boys and girls who must acquire the communication skills in order to compete for their daily bread, and become first class citizens and participants in the community, rather than the exploited minority.

For the colleges and universities of America, I invite a review of admissions standards and language requirements. Bilingual Americans should be accredited at college admission for their language proficiency rather than penalized as they presently are. Proficiency examinations should replace courses and credits that are meaningless most of the time anyway, and a committee of professional bilinguals should develop such examinations to avoid the predominance of traditionalism in our academic reforms. It is a national tragedy that bilingual Americans have not been granted entrance credit at the college or university of their choice, while the monolingual student is admitted without proficiency. This we have done in the name of the humanities and quality education. It is also a tragic fact that we have spent billions of dollars developing second and third language proficiencies, while we have discouraged the bilingual students from developing their domestic language since the primary grades. This must change. Counseling and curriculum experts must properly identify values and assets, and our tax-supported schools must respond more imaginatively to the needs of its citizens.

What contribution does bilingual and bicultural education make to the total curriculum? If nothing else, it creates a new awareness of people and their needs, and of their legitimate request for a curriculum that relates to them, and it makes the school the hub of community life where children will grow and find fulfillment. Spanish-speaking children learn to read faster and better, they stay in school longer, and they are now knocking on the door of the public college and university for admission. Bilingual and bicultural education is not a panacea for what ails Spanish-speaking and other minorities. But it is a material and substantive force in the struggle for quality education.

Who are the benefactors of bilingual and bicultural education? Everyone. First, those to whom we address our language and other learnings. Second, the school and community and all those who live in it and recognize communication as a basic American shortcoming. Third, the nation as a whole because fewer dropouts, more educational opportunities, more college and vocational students, are conjugated in higher productivity, higher salaries, more taxes, less welfare. Bilingual and bicultural education must be made an integral part of the mainstream of the school curriculum. America must open its doors to the creativity of its children, and it must open its heart to all children who beg admission.

4

COMMUNITY AS A PRODUCER OF EDUCATION
FOR CULTURAL PLURALISM:
CONFORMAL EDUCATION VS MUTUAL RESPECT

EUGENE SEKAQUAPTEWA

The American public school system universally has been based on the principle that all of the children of all of the people from many different ethnic backgrounds with many different degrees of motivation are to be accommodated. This principle has never really been practiced in American public schools or in higher education. Minority groups throughout the country in the past and in the present have had to isolate themselves culturally and educationally in an effort to assure their cultural survival. It is only recently that public institutions which are in existence for the purpose of influencing minority group education have begun to make an effort to deviate from the traditional system of public education. The latter is sometimes referred to as "conformal education."

Actually, public education in America has been based primarily on American middle-class cultural and racial ethnocentrism. Cultural pluralism must necessarily involve philosophical realignment as well as systematic approaches in educational programs and in the development of educational personnel if we are to achieve the goals that may be established to ensure cultural pluralism.

America is now witnessing a semblance of a trend that indicates a need to restructure its educational practices based on multicultural elements in an effort to resolve some of its social ills. Although this trend may be the result of injustices incurred by ethnic minorities because of current educational practices, it is apparent that American educators have realized that education for cultural pluralism can benefit people of all cultures in the community. We are now engaged in activities which will allow us to broaden the utilization of our educational resources to benefit the American community as a whole.

The teaching of cross-cultural understanding requires teachers who are adequately prepared to function in, and to accept, dissimilar cultural values. At the same time, the teacher needs to appreciate his role in his own culture. Before he can adequately understand another culture and its idiosyncracies, the teacher will need to take an objective look at his own.

In an effort to describe our national effort to effect teacher training programs for cross-cultural education, I feel it is appropriate to express concepts and principles in terms of the American Indian cultures that have survived systematic approaches designed to exterminate them.

Recently, much effort has been devoted to conducting workshops and other special training for teachers of Indian students. These efforts were generated primarily by the availability of federal funds and were organized by various schools or other special interest groups. However, there has been no evidence of any formal teacher training program for teachers of Indian students that developed from these workshops.

On the surface, it may appear that training teachers to teach pupils of specific ethnic origin is discriminatory. However, my observations have indicated that this approach has given the teacher an opportunity to become sensitive to cultural pluralism.

Arizona State University (ASU) is the only institution of higher education in this country that has developed, as part of its academic program, courses specifically designed to train teachers of Indian students. Although the Center for Indian Education at ASU has been in operation for more than a decade, it can only be described as being in its infancy in relation to needs that are evident in Indian education.

One of the observable by-products of ASU's program is that teachers who have been trained to teach Indian students are beginning to supplement their school curriculum with relevant information on local ethnic groups as well as to utilize available resources from local ethnic communities.

The ethnic communities as producers of education in America have always been suppressed by the concept called the melting-pot theory. In actuality, the melting-pot theory has never been practiced in American education; rather, European-American cultural values have always dominated the philosophical foundations of American education.

The methods and approaches of training teachers for cultural pluralism must necessarily involve development of curriculum and implementation of curriculum. The critical requirement for determining philosophical guidelines for the development of curriculum must be based on full participation of ethnic communities.

Some of the suggested approaches might include the following:

1. State and other government authorities must develop a system or vehicle which will enable the state universities to meet the needs for training teachers for cultural pluralism, i.e., centers for ethnic studies.
2. Local school districts must become sensitive to local ethnic communities and initiate steps to modify local school curricula based on the real educational needs of local ethnic groups.

In conclusion, the fact cannot be overemphasized that over a hundred American Indian cultures and languages form the foundation for Indian communities; therefore, the right of the Indian community, or any other ethnic community, to exist, to participate in, and to maintain its role in America must be the ultimate objective of all programs designed to initiate change in American education.

5

CULTURAL PLURALISM

DILLON PLATERO

Cultural pluralism and its implications for teaching in the nation's public and private schools is a phenomenon which has become almost a fad. To members of other clearly defined cultural groups, such as many American Indians, there is more than a touch of irony in observing the nonculturally differentiated mass clamor about the desirability of multicultural facility. The goals are those that we Indian peoples have found thrust upon us since time immemorial. We would hope, however, to assist in making such learnings less traumatic than they have been for our peoples.

One facet of cultural pluralism needs to be clearly understood at the beginning before one can expect to make progress in the area: Intercultural teachings must look upon both cultures as equally worthy, as equally due respect. Many programs founder on this issue before they really get started.

Rough Rock Demonstration School

At Rough Rock Demonstration School, in the heart of the Navajo Indian Reservation, cultural pluralism is a reality. It is a teaching area which receives constant attention.

The school itself is located in a complex of modern buildings constructed by the Bureau of Indian Affairs in 1965-1966 as a boarding school to accommodate elementary-school-age children in the Rough Rock community, a group of about 1,000 people scattered over a wide area. Just as the school was about to open its doors for the first time (replacing the old structure built in the 1930s) the community was given the unique opportunity to assume control over its operation in actual fact, as contrasted to widely touted but nonetheless impuissant advisory school boards which are "involved" at other schools on the reservation.

The community accepted the challenge and Rough Rock Demonstration School came into being. Since then the people of Rough Rock have gained immensely in self-confidence in their ability to operate their own school. We have added grade levels until we now boast of serving students from nursery school through the tenth grade. Plans are also going well toward the addition of the final two years of secondary education, and Rough Rock High School will graduate its first class in 1974.

In the elementary section (nursery school through grade five) we have eight Navajo teachers and five non-Indians. It thus becomes obvious that the concept of cultural pluralism readily can be practiced at this community's school, if such is deemed a worthy undertaking, which it is at Rough Rock.

Cultural Pluralism at Rough Rock

A prerequisite to understanding cultural pluralism as it exists at Rough Rock is an understanding of one of the basic premises upon which the school is founded: respect for the individual child and recognition of the need to instill self respect and self confidence in him.

How often on Indian reservations, at least on ones which have viable cultures of their own, have we found the indigenous culture/language denigrated and the new language/culture exalted by persons who are vicious at worst and well-meaning dupes at best. Let me make plain that the days of corporal punishment for speaking one's mother tongue at school are, by and large, gone. And just as overt physical action is frowned upon in response to such manifestations of use of one's native culture, so are more subtle forms of punishment. However, in myriad ways (and this can be accomplished without a word spoken in any language) Indian children are reminded of the inherent inferiority of their own language and culture and of the superiority of the culture and language of the culturally nondifferentiated mass.

The very fact that most beginning Indian students are met during their first year in school by teachers who do not speak their mother tongue, plus the fact that the teacher assumes a role of no small importance to the child during that first year, combine to create a feeling of cultural inferiority in the child without anyone necessarily really wanting such a result. An obvious way to combat such an insidious form of ethnocentrism would be to let a beginning student be instructed in the mother tongue by native speakers of the language. This is being done at Rough Rock during the first two grades.

Lest there be any doubt, it should be conceded here that our students learn early that there are two major cultures in their world, along with two major languages, and that their interactions with members of the other culture/language group must be modified to achieve the caliber of inter-personal relationships desired. All too often one gets the impression that children exist in culture-tight jars: one before beginning school and a different type of jar afterward. This is patently untrue because very early there is a combination of cultural traits in which the child grows—a third culture, as it were, to which the child becomes, of necessity, acclimated.

Using Title VII funds from the Elementary and Secondary Education Act, the Bilingual Program at Rough Rock attempts to bring to the forefront of educators' attention the fact that cultural pluralism, facility in another culture in addition to the one into which a person is born, is an advantage to the student.

This year (1971-1972), for the first time in the history of the school, we have an all-Navajo student body and thus our studies in this realm are rather one-sided and conform (as far as the student body is concerned) to what is expected of a cultural minority anyway: familiarity with the nonculturally differentiated mass.

Of great importance is the opposite: the familiarization of the mass with the culture of a minority. It is in this regard that the true test of the efficacy of such teaching comes. And in this regard one must admit to being somewhat less than optimistic. Illustrative is the situation that exists around almost every Indian reservation in the country, where the non-Indian residents of the towns know and appreciate so appallingly little about reservation culture. Oftentimes even a perverse negative knowledge is flaunted by those who do not feel too economically threatened by such action.

Near the Navajo reservation the town of Gallup has long represented all the worst in Indian/non-Indian relations. Although at the present time some small beginnings are being made by the dominant culture in becoming more knowledgeable about the language/culture of the reservation, it would appear that the most promising factor to give such actions a fillip will be growing economic power, selectively used, of the Indian people themselves.

Summary

As communications media daily continue their work of bringing the peoples of this nation more and more standardized fare, we find actual living refuting, to some degree, the desires of the minute segment of educators who are aware of the advantages that accrue to students who are accomplished in various cultural media.

As much as one hates to admit it, prognosis for the teaching of cultural pluralism without cultural condescension is not good. Although it may be the "in" thing to laud cultural pluralism, one must admit that realistically there may be nearly as much harm done as good while the members of various minority cultural groups become objects of the blunderings of the nonculturally differentiated mass which, however well intentioned, are still demeaning.

Essentially, then, we at Rough Rock are working from one side of the picture: to attempt to help our students become facile in the dominant culture as well as in their own mother culture. To do the reverse presents a more formidable problem, inasmuch as actual motivation is manifestly lacking in children of the dominant culture and almost never can be accomplished without harming persons of minority cultures in the process.

The understandings that arise from cultural awareness, from the end results of the teaching of cultural pluralism, are similar to seeing through a glass darkly: People of good will in the dominant culture may see less darkly but until they can discard their own fears and become able to accept themselves for what they are, they are not going to be doing anyone much real good by dabbling in cultural pluralism.

6

MAKING THE SCHOOLS A VEHICLE FOR CULTURAL PLURALISM

BARBARA A. SIZEMORE

Today the schools are in trouble. The youth are in rebellion. High schools are so chaotic in some places that they must close to reorganize. They reflect the society and the times since education is a product of that society and culture and is the deliberate or purposeful creation, evocation, or transmission of knowledge, abilities, skills, and values.

Silberman cites mindlessness as the cause of what is wrong with the public schools. He defines mindlessness as the failure or refusal to think seriously about educational purpose, the reluctance to question established practice. This analysis completely avoids the discussion of purposeful action, thereby eliminating forceful cultural imperatives such as racism. Consequently, Silberman falls victim to a classic educational error: the inaccurate definition of the problem.[1] Such inaccurate definitions lead to the wrong solutions. This paper will attempt to discuss (1) the meaning of culture, pluralism, and related concepts; (2) the values emanating from the culture; (3) the educational system produced by this value system; and (4) a model for change.

If the schools reflect the society and the culture, then certain cultural imperatives may operate as causes. In man's attempt to preserve and

[1] Charles E. Silberman, *Crisis in the Classroom* (New York: Random House, 1970).

reproduce himself, he has been in constant conflict with the land, nature, and other men. Sekou Toure defines culture as the "expression in particular and specific forms of a general problem—that of the relationships linking man to his environment."[2] These relationships are greatly affected by differentiations in the structure of the object world with regard to orientation to the polarity of gratification and deprivation.[3]

Egos interact with social objects called alters and with nonsocial objects. Social objects have expectations which are oriented toward egos producing a complementarity of expectations. This system can be analyzed in terms of the degree of conformity of ego's action with alter's expectations and vice versa, and the contingent reactions of alter to ego's action are sometimes called sanctions.

The effect of these sanctions is determined by ego's need-dispositions and the ability of alter to gratify or deprive. There, then, is a double contingency inherent in such interaction. Ego's gratifications are dependent on his selection among available alternatives and alter's reaction will be determined by ego's selection. This double contingency produces the precondition for cultural patterns. Thus complementarity of expectations in the processes of human interaction is central in the analysis of the cultural patterns.

In this social order where so many groups with varying cultural patterns reside, pluralism and desires for inclusion confound the double contingency and the complementarity of expectations. Pluralism is the condition of cultural parity among ethnic groups in a common society. Cruse says that "America is an unfinished nation—the product of a badly-bungled process of inter-group cultural fusion . . . [and] it has effectively dissuaded, crippled and smothered the cultivation of a democratic cultural pluralism in America."[4] Most excluded ethnic groups strive for inclusion or full participation in the social order with preservation of ethnic differences.[5] The obstacles to the attainment of inclusion are the institutions which

[2] Sekou Toure, "A Dialectical Approach to Culture," *The Black Scholar*, November, 1969, p. 13.

[3] The following discussion of culture was taken from Talcott Parsons and Edward A. Shils, eds., *Toward A General Theory of Action* (New York: Harper & Row, 1951), pp. 14-16.

[4] Harold Cruse, *The Crisis of the Negro Intellectual* (New York: William Morrow, 1967), p. 456.

[5] See Talcott Parsons, "Full Citizenship Rights for the Negro" in Talcott Parsons and Kenneth B. Clark, eds. *The Negro American*, (Boston: Houghton Mifflin, 1965), pp. 720-722.

perpetuate, promote, and preserve the symbolic systems of the dominant ethnic group (alter).

The great myth that the public schools were effective mobility vehicles for white American immigrant groups has been a notorious diehard.[6] Although many want to say that the schools did assist the various immigrants, they, in fact, did not. Most immigrants were excluded from effective participation in the contriently interdependent competitive model of capitalism through the economic paradigm of supply and demand in labor.[7]

If A represents groups with power and B represents groups with no power, this social order can be described as one where A has power over B (A/B). Capitalism working through the contriently interdependent competitive model creates a situation where when A wins, B loses and vice versa. Inherent in the model there will always be losers. The question is not will there be unemployment, but who will be unemployed? The problem for A is how to keep B in a powerless position. The problem for B is how to achieve a position of parity and power.

Previously excluded groups formed group mobility vehicles outside the public schools for they dared not depend on A institutions contrived to promote the best interest of A. Jewish groups pulled themselves up around the synagogue and the multitude of organizations and associations protecting the Jewish community. The Irish Catholics used the Roman Catholic Church. The Chinese had the tong; the Sicilians the Mafia. These models have been labeled Power-Inclusion Models.[8] Such a model has five stages, the first being the separatist position wherein the groups manifest an ideology consisting of: (1) a pseudo-species declaration which articulates the belief that the group is the chosen people of God; (2) a specific identity revealed in the name the group calls itself; and (3) a territorial imperative or homeland. In the second stage, that of nationalism, the group intensifies its "we groupness" through the negative identity which provides a way to project everything bad about the group onto another people. Additionally, in this stage the ideology created in the first stage is

---

[6] Silberman, op. cit., pp. 54-58.

[7] For a discussion of the contriently interdependent model see Morton Deutsch, "Cooperation and Trust: Some Theoretical Notes" in Warren G. Bennis et al., eds., *Interpersonal Dynamics* (Homewood Ill.: The Dorsey Press, 1964), pp. 564-582.

[8] Barbara A. Sizemore "Separatism: A Reality Approach to Inclusion?" in Robert L. Green, ed., *Racial Crisis in American Education* (Chicago: Follett Educational Corporation, 1969), pp. 249-279.

preserved and promoted by myths, rites and rituals, associations, organizations, and finally by institutions.

This institutional development sets the stage for the kind of aggregate power which creates work niches and economic blocs. In this phase the group monopolizes some skills or controls some entry levels into unions, businesses, or other endeavors, thereby assuring members of the group easy access to the structural slots known as jobs. This economic foundation leads to stage four, or pluralism, when the group is ready to make coalitions with other groups to form voting blocs and negotiation teams on a level of parity with other groups. The last stage is the stage of power.

The serious questions now being asked regarding cultural pluralism are urgent because the groups challenging the schools have either no ideology or no alternative institutions for support. Either the public schools must do it or else. But how can one make the schools a vehicle for inclusion? If A group is alter and B group represents ego, wherein B's gratifications are contingent on its selection among available alternatives, then A's reaction will be contingent on B's selection and will result from a complementary selection on A's part. If the values and norms of A groups are the norms of all groups, this means that the schools will be used to maintain the power for A since A controls them. How can the operation of such institutions result from mindlessness, when they serve to maintain power? If one rejects the argument of mindlessness, then one must face the thought that this refusal to question educational practice is a purposeful act.

If man acts for a reason, then his actions have purpose. According to Parsons and Shils, behavior is oriented to the attainment of ends or goals. Behavior takes place in situations and is normatively regulated. Additionally, it involves expenditure of energy or effort or motivation.[9] Such behaviors are called actions. Actions occur in constellations which are called systems. The schools are social systems, or systems of action, which have a process of interaction between two or more actors and where this concert is a function of collective goal orientation, or common values, and of a consensus of normative and cognitive expectations. Collective goal orientation, or common values guide the choices, then, that the actors make.

Using Kluckhohn and others, a value is a conception, explicit or implicit, distinctive of an individual or characteristic of a group, of the desirable which influences the selection from available modes, means, and

---

[9] Parsons and Shils, op. cit., p. 53.

ends of action.[10] Values can become the large-ended goal statements of a society. Norms, standards, laws, rules, and regulations are devised to support these values or large-ended goal statements. Individuals are motivated to comply with the standards, to meet the norms, and to obey the laws, rules, and regulations. Situational factors provide the knowledge, skills, and information which motivate the individuals to comply with the norms and to obey the laws which uphold the values or large-ended goal statements. Schools are one of the many institutions which provide this knowledge and these skills and information, and values organize the systems of action.

What values organize schools? Ordinarily one thinks of achievement, respect for property, democracy, love, peace, and brotherhood. The school certainly stresses these goal statements. Why then do certain groups fail to achieve, to respect property, and to observe democracy, love, peace, and brotherhood? Why does the theory of action outlined by Parsons and Shils fail to apply to public schools? These questions create an interesting field of inquiry.

If achievement is a value, it is desirable and influences selection. When violated, it causes guilt, shame, self-depreciation, ego diminution, or it evokes severe negative social sanctions.[11] But, in this social order, certain groups evoke severe negative social sanctions when they work hard. For example, Black people worked in slavery from 1619 through 1865 and received nothing as remuneration, not even a chance to run for the land when Oklahoma was opened up. The legendary forty acres and a mule never materialized. In fact, the emancipated Blacks were returned to slavery by the deal made for a Republican president in the first Reconstruction. Presently, Black people who graduate from college still receive less pay than whites with high school educations.[12] Furthermore, desegregation models in the South are displacing Black teachers and creating restless new reservoirs of Black unemployment.[13]

In fact, democracy is more difficult to find no matter what definition one uses—government vested in the people or political and social equality.

[10] Clyde Kluckhohn and others, "Values and Value-Orientations in the Theory of Action: An Exploration in Definition and Classification" in Parsons and Shils, op. cit., p. 395.

[11] Ibid., pp. 407-408.

[12] Thomas Johnson, "Returns from Investment in Human Capital," *American Economic Review*, September, 1970, p. 558.

[13] Robert Hooker, "Integration Cheats Black Teachers," *Chicago Sun-Times*, January 10, 1971, sec. 2, pp. 2-3.

Does Congress represent the poor? The young? The Blacks? Or women? Whom does Congress represent? Why do oilmen get oil depletion allowances and some millionaires pay no income taxes? Why are suburban homes subsidized and inner city residences "urban-renewed?" What institutions uphold the value of democracy?

Moreover, if values do not pass the tests of guilt evocation and sanctions, are they values? Kluckhohn and others hasten to say that one dares not assume *ex hypothesi* that verbal behavior tells the observer less about the "true" values than other types of action, for both verbal and nonverbal acts must be carefully studied.[14] Therefore, let us concede for the sake of the argument that achievement, respect for property, democracy, love, peace, and brotherhood are verbal values upheld by the norms but not characterized by conformity in action.

In fact, Wheelis argues that there are two kinds of values: institutional and instrumental. The former are derived from myths, mores, and status and transcend the evidence at hand; the latter are derived from tool-using, observation, and experimentation and are ordered by the former. If this is so, then another set of values may order, direct, organize, and integrate the values of achievement, property, love, democracy, peace, and brotherhood.[15] These institutional values may be male superiority, white European superiority, and the superiority of people with money, especially since nearly every institution in this social order and most norms, standards, laws, rules, and regulations support these three values while instantly creating three disadvantaged groups: women, Blacks and non-Europeans, and the poor. Groups disadvantaged by the value system and its concomitant norms, standards, rules, regulations, and laws must change the educational system which disadvantages them.

The plain truth is that black people have inaccurate conceptual maps of reality. Another fact is that A groups (alter) control the distribution and dissemination of knowledge in order to preserve certain symbolic universes. The knowledge produced is institutionalized through certain behavior typification systems which are then internalized by individuals to maintain certain groups in excluded and/or inferior positions.

These sets of knowledge preserve the values also. America is depicted often in the curriculum as democratic but seldom as capitalistic. Since the

---

[14] Kluckhohn and others, op. cit., p. 406.

[15] Allen Wheelis, *The Quest for Identity* (New York: W. W. Norton, 1958), p. 179. See also Barbara A. Sizemore, "Social Science and the Black Identity" in James A. Banks and Jean D. Grambs, eds., *Black Self-Concept* (New York: McGraw-Hill, 1971).

country has not yet achieved democracy, the schools should teach the citizens the capitalistic structure so they can understand how it works and can use it to help themselves. Moreover, since food, housing, clothing, and medicine are for sale in this country at a profit, certainly the poor and the disadvantaged first should be taught how to make money. Yet, scarcely a word is said about economics except in the sense of consumership. In fact, Jules Henry states that the purpose of education is just that—to make people buy![16]

More to the point, schools where the disadvantaged are educated have programs for training in obsolete skills and trades. Few schools train or educate the poor and the disadvantaged in technology or the hard sciences. Few trade schools offer programs for apprenticeship in the building trades. More than likely, Blacks are prohibited from obtaining apprenticeships. Most training for such jobs nowadays occurs on the job. The problem for Blacks and women is how to get on the job!

The educational curriculum is dominated by white European feats, exploits, and miracles. Christopher Columbus discovered America even though the people he incorrectly named Indians were already here. Man began in the Caucasus Mountains, but the earliest bones of man were found in Olduvai Gorge, Kenya, East Africa. The history of the Black people in America began in 1619, yet they had a homeland in Africa before that time. All kinds of European interpretations strangle Black dreams and aspirations. The Constitution guarantees liberty, equality, and the pursuit of happiness. But, when Blacks agitate for these guarantees, sociologists scream "rising expectations" and "benign neglect."

If culture does indeed provide the standards which are applied in evaluative processes, and if culture is an expression of a general problem—that of the relationships linking man to his environment—then B groups can no longer allow A groups to define their problems, create their values, and devise their norms. Otherwise the motivational and situational factors which work toward uniformities in codes and standards, trends in action such as striving and energy disposal, and choices and interests, will continue to preserve and maintain the system of B group exclusion and cultural denigration.

A decision-making apparatus assuring B group participation and power is needed to establish a mutually shared symbolic system in the complementarity of expectations and the double contingency. This is a necessity in institutions shaping the life chances of B groups. Numerous mechanisms

[16] Jules Henry, *Culture Against Man* (New York: Random House, 1963).

must be designed to afford the opportunities of a multitude of interactions among the personalities and roles within the social system of the school. These interactions act as inputs which will affect the outputs by bringing the values of the institution in line with the values of the clients.

An aggregate model is needed to accomplish these goals.[17] Such a model must give each role and group a position of parity and power in the decision-making. B groups need not feel that A groups will willingly succumb or surrender these powerful institutions which keep them in power. The control of these institutions will result from repeated struggles, conflicts, and confrontations. A groups will design programs to absorb the energies of B groups and to displace the liberation goals with survival goals. A groups will co-opt B groups and B group programs so that they veer from the original directions and point toward A group goals and ends. This is to be expected since A groups are in power. However, the struggle must go on. The change will be effective if the values are no longer acknowledged and/or respected. Alternate symbolic universes will be legitimatized if the people so decide.

Such a school which is a vehicle for cultural pluralism would operate from an aggregate model rather than a specialization model. One such model is CAPTS,[18] designed and implemented in the Woodlawn Experimental Schools District Project (WESP), an Elementary and Secondary Education Act (ESEA), Title III government-funded project under Public Law 89-10 in Chicago. This project is operated under a tripartite arrangement with three institutions: The Woodlawn Organization, The University of Chicago, and the Chicago Board of Education. The district is governed by the Woodlawn Community Board which has twenty-one members, ten from The Woodlawn Organization, seven from the Chicago Board of Education, and four from The University of Chicago. The Woodlawn Community Board makes policy for the district. However, it is only a recommending body as the Chicago Board of Education retains approval-veto powers.

The district, located in Woodlawn, one of the ten poorest of the seventy-five city community areas, has three components: the community component, the research and evaluation component, and the in-school component. It has three schools: Hyde Park High School, Wadsworth Elementary School, and Wadsworth Upper Grade Center. The community

[17]Morris Janowitz, "Institution Building in Urban Education" in David Street, ed., *Innovations in Mass Education* (New York: John Wiley, 1969), pp. 273-342.

[18]CAPTS: C = Community representative   A = Administrators   P = Parents
T = Teachers   S = Students

component has twenty-five community agents who organize and convene some forty parent councils of approximately twenty members each. These parent councils each elect a president or chairman who sits on the Woodlawn Parent Council Advisory Board. These members become alternates for Woodlawn Community Board members. These parent council presidents attend leadership training sessions to learn how to be a Board member, how to use Robert's *Rules of Order*, and how to understand school law, Board rules, and other necessary information.

The in-school component has forty community teachers (teachers' aides). These community teachers and parents attend workshops in methods of teaching the Ethnolinguistic Cultural Approach to Oral Language and the Sensory-Motor-Perceptual Program. Community teachers have learned to test and screen for the latter program and many of them know how to teach the first rudiments of reading skills. Moreover, parents have been trained for positions as community agents, community teachers, and research assistants, and they serve in classrooms on teams to solve problems.

The primary objective of the WESP is to restructure the social system through a mutuality of effort by subsequent interventions which have two foci: (1) to change the roles and relationships in the school and (2) to change the roles and relationships in the community. The project is not only interested in who works together, but how. To the degree that the mutuality of effort effects a restructuring of the social system, the following secondary objectives are to be achieved: (1) elevation of achievement scores, (2) an improvement in self-concept, (3) a reduction in alienation, and (4) a sense of power over one's destiny. Mutuality of effort was to be achieved through CAPTS, and the CAPTS-WESP Decision-Making Model was to be the vehicle to restructure the social system and to produce cultural pluralism in WESP.

The Model has nine steps (see Figure 1). Program planning occurs in the CAPTS Congress. First, each group meets separately. A plan emerges from a group. It is submitted to the other groups, who discuss and negotiate. The negotiated plan is then sent to the professional bureaucracy to be formulated into an educational program. This formulation is sent to the administrative staff for organization. The administrative staff then submits the proposal to the Woodlawn Community Board (WCB). The WCB recommends or does not recommend. If WCB recommends and the proposal does not warrant submission to the Chicago Board of Education (CBE) (this means it does not infringe upon the power of the CBE), the proposal then comes back to the administrative staff for coordination and

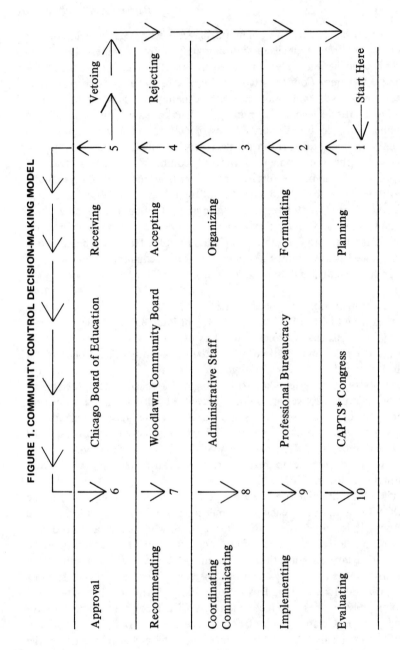

FIGURE 1. COMMUNITY CONTROL DECISION-MAKING MODEL

*CAPTS: Community, Administration, Parents, Teachers, Students

communication, to the professional bureaucracy for implementation, and back to the CAPTS Congress for evaluation. Each group first meets separately to discuss the method and the instruments to be used for evaluation. These are then negotiated and the evaluation takes place according to the negotiated plan. If a proposal or plan fails to be recommended by the WCB or is vetoed by the CBE it returns to the CAPTS Congress and starts over again.

Implementing cultural pluralism demands the input which an aggregate model provides. It needs the diagnostic skills of the professional staff. In such a school, diagnosis would be the important program. Teachers would need to become skilled in techniques of data collection and analysis, such as interviewing, microethnography, questionnaire construction, public opinion polling, test construction, categorizing, and codification. Diagnosis would not stop nor necessarily start in the classroom but would encompass the entire community, especially as it related to the student's present, past, and future existence. It would need administrators amenable to the collective decision-making model described above or administrators willing to share power.

More important, excluded groups cannot conform to A group's system of "ways of orienting" and B groups must project their new external symbols to control new ways of orienting so that the new system will be geared into the action systems of both A and B. The construction and maintenance of the public school system is far from mindless. It is purposeful, directed toward the preservation of B group's conformity to A group's norms and values.

To make the schools a vehicle for cultural pluralism, the institutional values of male superiority, white European superiority, and the superiority of people with money must be abandoned. Secondly, education must be for the purpose of self-fulfillment and self-realization by the expansion of the human potential for the best possible interests of each person concerned so that he can lead a more meaningful life in a democracy for the betterment of himself and all mankind.

Next, a new all-human ethic must be employed. One that could be tried is that of the "Golden Talent." The basic assumption is that people are different. Each person is predisposed toward a certain approach to learning. Some people are sight learners, some kinesthetic, some auditory; some are abstract thinkers, some manipulate ideas, some memorize. In fact, there may be as many approaches to learning as there are people. But everyone has a talent. Observations of these will dictate what is taught to that learner. This curriculum will not be obstructed by racist and/or chauvinist values.

There is no doubt that a democratic culturally pluralistic society is imperative. That fights must be waged on all fronts is accepted. Let Americans tell no more lies, make no more myths, create no more evasions like integration and desegregation, revenue sharing and voucher systems. At long last, let's set about to cure the disease and not treat the symptoms. Education can be concerned then with the meeting of men's needs of identity, stimulation, and security based on the values of land, liberty, and life. Once this occurs, the vital area of man's purpose and existence on this earth becomes the primary focus of his educational experience and the point position at the frontier of knowledge.

7

THE RELATIONSHIPS BETWEEN THE UNIVERSITY AND THE COMMUNITY IN THE DEVELOPMENT OF CULTURAL PLURALISM

CYRIL D. TYSON

When one embarks upon a journey into the world of education, he must know the road he is going to travel, know where it leads, and be sure of the objectives at the end. I anticipate your journey with me as I share with you my notions on the "Relationships between the University and the Community in the Development of Cultural Pluralism." I am aware that in order to maximize the possibility of success the major and often controversial terms in the topic title should be defined beforehand.

Cultural pluralism is the belief in, and the coexistence of, people from diverse cultural backgrounds who accept and practice the notion that to be different is not to be inferior. Those who commit themselves to this belief agree that the old ethnocentric approach to religious, national, and racial groups cannot be validated. They accept the intrinsic worth of all human beings and understand that the learning of new patterns of behavior is not necessarily inconsistent with the maintenance of other desired norms, traits, or elements of lifestyle. Individuals who function in such an environment will have the opportunity to develop positive self-images, and will tend to take on and give up elements of culture in nondefensive ways. They will preserve cultural patterns through group and institutional affiliations that provide adequate avenues of expression and they will alter their lifestyle through membership in other groups and through different insti-

[55

tutional affiliations that provide the opportunity for shared experiences around activities of mutual interest.

A community is a collection of individuals, groups, and institutions that are usually located in a definable geographic area. It can also be a specific institution whose value system is expressed through individual member participation in its activities, or through the activities of other groups and institutions in and outside of the geographic area. During the growth of urban communities the identification of community has become a difficult process. The urban individual belongs to and affiliates with many more groups, organizations, institutions, and publics than his rural counterpart. Within this pattern of relationships he performs a variety of roles through which he represents his concerns and individual and group aspirations.

Such an individual might agree with proponents on a civic issue in his role as a member of a fraternal organization and disagree or remain silent as the officer of his local union when the issue is put before the group. He might express his position on a critical issue consistent with the view of his religious organization, but privately vote contrary to that position when the issue comes before his professional organization. This does not mean that those who support full community participation in the decision-making process on issues that affect their well-being will not secure an adequate response. It does mean that consensus that can be sustained over long periods of time is more difficult to achieve. This is true because of the varied avenues and ways in which expression is forthcoming and the rapidity with which feelings on issues might change depending on the issues' effect on individual values or institutional domain.

The university is an institution of higher education that is usually composed of colleges, graduate schools, research centers, institutes, and programs that are general and specialized. It differs from an undergraduate school or college in a variety of ways. For the purpose of this paper the difference I will emphasize is its political organization. By the university's political organization, I mean the size, structure, and membership of its board of trustees; its administrative structure, that is, responsibilities and power vested in department heads, deans, and faculty committees; and the source of its major endowments. While often a function of size, the organizational structure of the university is important because of the semi-autonomous nature of some of its own constituent parts and the ability or inability of the university to be responsive to those that it perceives to be its publics.

My observations will, to a limited degree, be applicable to the college. I am thoroughly aware that student teaching begins in college and that teacher trainers and others that affect the quality of the teaching profession are often located outside of the formal university system.

I am not assuming that everyone agrees with the definitions that have been set forth. I am assuming that if there are major differences with my view of reality, in the best educational tradition those who disagree will begin from where I am to persuade me to where they want me to go.

From its inception, the university has functioned to serve those institutions of society that demanded, either for reasons of professionality or status, that individuals be educated in order for them to be accepted within existing and developing professions. This service has also been extended to social or business and industry structures on behalf of those eligible for roles and positions within them by virtue of heredity and family standing. Historically, the pattern of university development has been cyclic, ranging from passively serving the ruling class, to being a locus of student political activism, to undergoing periods of governmental control depending on the country and the nature of the political structure, to a return to serving the ruling class. Over time, however, the student body has broadened to include the middle and lower middle class as more occupational positions have come to require the credentialization process.

In the United States the early institutions of higher education originated from religious institutions. There were later creations under the land-grant college legislation. The Eastern institutions of earlier vintage were structured more on the European model. The institutions of the Midwest and Far West reflected the agrarian nature of the country and were not colleges, as we now know them, until the nineteenth century.

Over time the university has very slowly, almost imperceptibly, broadened its services to meet the need of more publics. In recent years, there has been a growing demand for a rapid intensification of this process. Often some members of the university community have resisted these demands, perceiving in them a threat to the university as a center of research, educational excellence, and contemplation. They have voiced dire warnings of ultimate educational mediocrity. They overlook, in their effort to protect access to the institutions that keep the seals of credentials, the existence of a credential gap, a gap between knowledge acquired for certification and the knowledge required to perform specific tasks of the many professions and occupations which require certification. In addition, they forget that institutional centers of research came into existence comparatively late in the development of universities and not only in the university setting. Universities have not always been centers of objectivity and "the scientific method" as it relates to all aspects of human endeavor. More often than not they were instruments of maintaining the status quo, and in comparison to other institutions around them, rather conservative.

We are now witnessing a period of time in which the university is under attack from a variety of sources. Early attacks centered in urban communities where the universities were in the process of expansion. Often this expansion took place at the expense of the people in poverty who were residing contiguous to the boundaries of the university. Usually the poor were not aware of the extent of real-estate holdings by the university or for that matter that the university was often the landlord twice removed. As it became clear that the poor would not be able to locate satisfactory living facilities elsewhere at rentals they would be able to afford, they cried out against the expansion program of the universities. There were other attacks that related to the fact that those same institutions could adjoin or be surrounded by poverty and squalor, and yet at no time view themselves as having any responsibility to bring their expertise or influence to bear to help solve those problems. In fact, they often felt they were the aggrieved parties.

Universities utilized the poverty communities as laboratories for their graduate and undergraduate students who would study and analyze and write dissertations on specific problems that beset those communities. In no way did the university, politically or as an organized institution, view itself as having any responsibility to provide leadership that would direct the bringing about of basic changes in the life of the residents. Aside from the resources inherent in the variety of disciplines they housed, they did not relate, even in the most narrow context, to the educational problems of their neighboring communities.

It happens often in the struggle for justice that the oppressed, in articulating their needs, inform the larger society of its own dissatisfactions with its institutions and thus clarify basic needs for society as a whole. It was primarily the action of Blacks, voting in the legislative bodies of the Southern states during the Reconstruction period, that gave us public education. As a result, for the first time poor white people had access to educational opportunities. The adverse reaction to the war in Indochina by university students is the end process of a disaffection that started when many students realized that they came out of our universities ill-equipped to understand or cope with the expressions of desire for full equality that erupted from the Black, Puerto Rican, Mexican-American, and Indian communities in our land. The students, middle class and predominantly white, were jolted into a larger look at their university experience. They attacked the lack of relevancy, undemocratic procedures, and what they perceived to be alliances on the part of the universities with publics that were contributors to the existing social pathology.

If I have heard the activist students correctly—and I *have* listened to them—it seems to me what they are saying is simply this: As our society and our economy have grown more sophisticated and complex, the purpose of education in America has increasingly become universal vocational training. This process has subtly reshaped the priorities of American education to adapt it to the priorities of government and the private economy. In the current context, those priorities are repugnant and unacceptable to a vast segment of our young people. Our law schools have been grinding out lawyers trained primarily in property law. Our scientific and engineering schools have reflected the demands of the defense industry. Our architects learn to design that which it is profitable to build—which does not include, I might add, low-cost housing.[1]

So what comes forth quite clearly as a central issue is what is the purpose of a university at this stage of history and who should be the participants in making the decisions that will direct its future activity. There are some people in and out of the university community who feel that the university cannot be all things to all people and serve a variety of masters because then it will serve no one. Some of those who express this feeling believe that the university's primary responsibility is to educate individuals, conduct research, and to some degree aid in the preservation of culture. They define any other activity as either peripheral or irrelevant to the university's primary role.

It seems to me that is not a satisfactory answer. I think the questions that are being raised relate to the need for defining the substance of the educational process, of research, and application. They relate to the notion that keeping open the dialectics of culture is more appropriate than preserving it, static, at any point in time. The educational process must develop and maintain the environment for responding to what is occurring in a society that is becoming increasingly more complex, and in which many more occasions for interdependency are coming to the fore.

The university must learn to utilize in positive and productive ways the larger community of which it is a part. In order for this process to occur, the university must perceive that the community has something of value to

[1] From a speech by Richard G. Hatcher, Mayor of Gary, Indiana, presented at the Institute for Black Elected Officials, sponsored by the Metropolitan Applied Research Center, in Washington, D.C., September, 1969.

offer it, and the community must perceive that it has something of value to offer the university. It is within the context of a shared understanding of equal goals and objectives that some rational discourse will occur on how the universities and the communities might work together.

We learned in New York City, rather belatedly, that we made a mistake over the years when we attempted to bring about educational reform in the primary and secondary school system by pinpointing some problems in the way the Board of Education went about the business of educating our youth. Petitioning, even though backed up by educational analysis, did not bring about change. We came to understand that our view of the educational system in those terms was rather naive. We learned that the educational system in the first instance was a politicality, that it had a number of competing publics it had to accommodate, and that it was best understood via political analysis. It was necessary to understand economics and marketing in order to assess correctly the Board of Education's decisions that were made in the areas of school construction, purchasing of educational equipment, building renovations, and building maintenance. We finally recognized that primary and secondary education is a $2 billion business, and any educational reform that threatens existing patterns of distribution of those resources will be difficult to achieve.

It appears that the same kind of analysis, with more profound implications, pertain to the universities. Such an analysis will aid us in determining what is or is not possible in any attempt to develop productive relationships with communities. While universities will state that they are above politics and decry any but an objective approach to issues that come before them, the universities, by action and inaction, are involved in the political decision-making process. Decisions to expand or not to expand, to acquire additional land in one direction or the other, are political decisions—not just educational ones. Decisions to receive endowments from certain sources, in support of one program or another, are political as well as educational decisions. When one looks at the total budget of many of our major universities, inclusive of operating and capital funds, it becomes increasingly clear that the universities are big business under varying degrees of influence from the publics from which they derive their support.

The mechanism for imposing these priorities has also been discovered. No student is ever told outright that he must major in Business Administration or Aeronautical Engineering. Rather business and government together, through an intricate network of scholarships, research grants, summer jobs, loans for new building construction, and other forms of subsidies and inducements, cause certain academic disciplines to flourish while others are allowed to wither.[2]

If there are to be positive strategies of community involvement with and influence on universities, accurate information about the university ·and the community must be made available to both parties.

I think that Robert Ross is correct when he indicates that the universities play a strategic role in our contemporary American society, and that the role in large measure is to aid in the extension of large-scale corporate capitalism and to produce individuals who will preserve a social organization compatible with that system's well-being. Often those graduates who are successful in such endeavors will reward the universities with endowments or other financial contributions that help to make quite clear the importance of such a role. The universities are involved with society and have power. Power is never quite neutral. The real question is power and involvement "for whose interest, in what cause, and with what consequences for our common humanity."[3] The benchmark that must be applied is whether the universities or other institutions are structured and function in ways that enhance the continued development of the democratic ethic. Are their activities and programs keeping that process open and viable or are they contributing to the kinds of pressures that close out options critical for the survival of our democracy?

It is within this context that I view the relationship between the university and the community in the development of cultural pluralism. There must be some agreement between the universities and the community on what cultural pluralism is and what its place is within higher education. If there is consensus, the universities must organize themselves in a way in which there is maximum opportunity for this value to permeate their activities and programs. If this is possible, the university might then become more "egalitarian both in its admission policies and its so-called service functions. It would be committed to the redistribution of power and services . . . . The struggle for black liberation would not plague it but offer a university a vast opportunity to deliver on its moral promises."[4]

Let me emphasize that the sustaining values inherent in cultural pluralism will not evidence themselves because a special course is given here and

---

[2] Ibid.
[3] Robert Ross, "The University and the Future," *Social Policy*, November/December, 1970.
[4] Ibid.

there in different departments, or because some special program is attached as an appendage to the business-as-usual university. Special ethnically integrated advisory groups that are the sole attempt to actively involve appropriate representatives of the community in a meaningful relationship to the university are an unreal exercise in cultural pluralism. The values inherent in cultural pluralism will be expressed through a conscious administrative policy and structural design that fosters and defines as an academic good the active participation of those cultural communities and the university faculty in a real educational process.

Of course, the universities have not simply stood by while communities and students have been expressing their dissatisfaction. Some universities have developed programs and facilities out in the community that have permitted them to extend their resources and opportunities, as well as learn in a more direct way the concerns and aspirations of the community. Other universities have developed new programs in their existing facilities and encouraged the communities to enroll and participate in their expanded curricula.

There has been an acute financing problem, with the federal government and foundations being solicited to supplement the resources of the university. Most of the financing is on a year-to-year basis with three- and five-year grants being the exception and not the rule. There are some universities that are currently indicating that certain programs will have to be curtailed or cut back if additional and continuing funds are not made available. At Harvard University, two summer programs for minorities need funds in order to continue.[5] The Intensive Summer Studies Program which helps to increase the number of Black and other minority groups pursuing higher degrees in the arts and sciences might disappear because of the lack of funds. The Faculty Audit Program, an adjunct of the Intensive Summer Studies Program for faculty from Black colleges, is also in danger of closing. The program began in 1966, and Columbia and Yale Universities participated in 1967. Now only a small number of students remain in the program attending Harvard University.

Many of you remember the story of the Street Academy and Harlem Prep School in New York City.[6] These were sponsored by the New York Urban League. Youth used the street academies as a place to study and learn in order to enter the prep school. The prep school had a unique curriculum inclusive of Black studies. Of the prep school graduates 90

[5] *Harvard University Gazette* LXVI, 23 (February 26, 1971).
[6] *New York Times*, March 6, 1971.

percent went on to college. The street academies were supported by businesses when they were worried about riots. No notion of sustaining support of an individual through the entire process of education was considered. There is general agreement that the programs were successful; however, there are no funds to sustain them on a continuing basis as a new option for those who do aspire but require a different educational setting prior to entering college.

I relate these examples, and I know there are many more that you know from your personal experiences, because I think that the programs have to be institutionalized if they are to be an effective force for the community and the university. The situation raises some serious questions as to the sincerity of some public and private agencies and organizations that verbalize their concerns about the problems in America being solved through an educational approach. Many of them are not prepared to finance the process in a way that ensures success. I am not advocating that every experiment in university-community educational partnership become immediately institutionalized forever in the university. I am stating that the university must have a dependable source of funds, inclusive of redirected internal fiscal resources, in order for it to plan effectively over time for this broadened role and responsibility. As long as the programs, in or out of the university, are perceived, structured, and administered as temporary add-ons and a response to a limited hostile situation, no meaningful partnership can evolve.

There are many examples of success and failure in this new educational approach across the country. There is one example of a beginning success that I will share with you because of my intimate involvement with the program's development.

The City University of New York is perhaps the first university in the country to participate fully in a comprehensive manpower system. Its network of junior colleges located in each of the City's five boroughs provides basic education, English as a second language, high school equivalency preparation, and skill training courses in eleven Opportunity Centers that are part of that system. The comprehensive manpower system is administered by the Manpower and Career Development Agency of the Human Resources Administration. The Opportunity Centers are in regions that encompass the twenty-six poverty areas of the City. The recruitment, intake, testing, counseling, and referral are the responsibilities of twenty-six Neighborhood Manpower Service Centers that are under contract to the Manpower Agency through the Community Action Agencies. The Community Action Agencies have policy boards that are democratically elected by the residents of the target communities that have been defined as poverty areas by the Council Against Poverty, the board that makes policy and allocates federal and municipal poverty funds.

The colleges participate in this program in facilities that house other government agencies and community organizations that are also providing specific services in the comprehensive manpower system. The population being served are welfare recipients, high school dropouts, the chronically unemployed, minority underemployed, and employable handicapped. These groups are generally considered the lowest quartile of the labor force and the most difficult to train and place in employment. Over 75 percent of the enrollees are Black and Puerto Rican, with the percentage being a little lower for direct job placements.

The City University has recently implemented an open enrolment program in which all high school graduates can now attend its colleges. The persons in the manpower training programs who receive their high school equivalency diploma have equal access with others for entrance into the colleges. The program will measurably increase the Black and Puerto Rican participation in higher education.

In addition, the City University provides the educational training for all of the participants in the Public Service Career Program that is adminis- tered by the Manpower Agency. A major portion of the individuals completing their initial training and high school equivalency have entered the City University through the junior colleges, taking courses toward a two-year degree or in preparation for entrance into the four-year colleges that are a part of the system. What is important is that a program has been established that maximizes options and provides the opportunity to suc- ceed for those who were in many cases the rejects of the secondary school system. Educationally, their cultural backgrounds are utilized as an asset and not perceived as a liability.

With such a commitment on the part of the City University, it can develop and sustain new forms of institutional relationships with govern- ment agencies on the state and municipal levels and with the community. No attempt is made to mold a synthetic American but to increase the options for developing new life styles and the opportunities for cultural expression.

Let me now set forth fourteen recommendations that, if implemented, will have some positive effect on the ability of the university and the community to create the conditions under which a culturally pluralistic society can evolve.

I will begin with the university because it is the institution being questioned as to its relevancy while having a vested position of educational and economic power in its community. The way in which it exercises its prerogatives has a profound effect upon the community.

1. The procedure for governing the university must provide guidelines for consideration of the social and political effects of its policy decisions. There was a period when a decision by the university did not contribute to the closing out of options for individuals and groups who were adversely affected by the decision. Today this is less often the case, particularly in the urban centers of our society.

For example, at one time university expansion displaced individuals who, for the most part, could exercise other residential options. In our major cities, universities are increasingly being surrounded by poor people "of minority extraction" who have experienced decades of continuous segregation, discrimination, and total exploitation. Today, not only have the buildings they live in been allowed to deteriorate as part of the university expansion process, but they have no other viable options for better living. They are pawns in a larger economic game that is played out through real-estate manipulation. The university must finally recognize this fact and must, in designing its physical plant, encompass the needs of the residential community that all projections tell us will increase numerically in our central cities.

Social and political consequences flow from investment decisions. This truism can no longer be ignored. The university will have to decide how it uses its influence, reflected in its corporate portfolio, to insure that its corporate activity, in the name of free enterprise, does not inhibit the development of democracy. To be silent is to make a choice. In the financial world, everyone knows that not to vote in a proxy fight is to support existing management. This means that the university must be aware of and sensitive to the investment and employment practices of the corporations in its portfolio as well as its own direct activities in these areas.

For example, if the university supports minority economic development as a social and economic good, it must perceive that the judicious placement of its bank deposits can play an enormously effective role in this development. Such deposits could strengthen the ability of an integrated or minority controlled banking institution to aid in the generation of necessary risk capital in order to develop poor communities. Or the university could determine which of the banks that are repositories of its funds loan to minority businessmen on an equal basis or cooperate with the Small Business Administration loan program. An institution cannot through its research and study contribute to a greater understanding of societal direction and, still as a center of power and influence, selectively use that power and influence in ways that are detrimental to those understandings. Those who are poor and exploited would have a right to say that such institutions should not be exempt from taxes because the only way a portion of those institutional resources are available to the community is through taxation.

2. The university must give recognition and credit toward professional advancement to all of those who implement action programs as they do to those who publish. The publish or perish syndrome must be moderated. We know that it is possible to produce material that does not increase our knowledge or understanding and still move up on the institutional ladder of success. I am not saying that those who increase our knowledge through publication of their works should not be rewarded. It seems to me, however, that those who choose to demonstrate their understanding and knowledge through direct involvement with the social issues of our times, by contributing to the implementation of significant programs that further desired goals and objectives, should have equal promise of academic advancement.

There are some social scientists who are better able to translate and transfer their ideas into immediately productive programs that are currently needed, than to take one or two years to write them up. Frequently, a thesis of innovative significance can no longer be validated through implementation at the time and place of the year of publication. The university can ill afford to absolve itself of responsibility for the non-use of its research findings or publications. It must reconstruct the process of inquiry to be inclusive of appropriate collaborative efforts that will maximize the effective use of findings. This involves the redefinition of the substance of the research process as well as of the nature of the participants in that process.

The critical domestic and international issues of our time come into focus and are sharpened as they are expressed by national, cultural, racial, and even religious groups or communities. A recognition of this pluralistic condition, and of its importance academically, might encourage the university to reevaluate the criteria by which it defines worthwhile activity in these areas. The rapid rate of change does not permit the normal process of data gathering and information dissemination to be relevant to the publics in our communities. Increased support of action research and direct involvement of the university community in implementation of programs will increase the credibility of the faculty and the university in the eyes of the community.

On many occasions, members of the university community have participated in activities and programs in areas of corporate and governmental collaboration with resultant personal financial reward and university recognition. Those engaged in similar approaches with community groups are engaging with problems of equal if not greater complexity, of equal if not greater significance to the survival of the democratic process, and should be similarly honored.

3. The university should be a source of technical assistance that enables the community to develop the methodology and techniques to institutionalize its knowledge and capabilities as a marketable commodity. Universities, other institutions, and government have often designed and participated in structures and administrative procedures to protect those groups in society that are exploited. The commissions that study social injustice, agencies that investigate discriminatory practices, and procedures that regulate abuses are not the structures that will in the long run account for the survival of democracy. The university, as the symbolic repository of the highest in intellectual activity and action, can *honestly* enter into the dialectic of democracy only by encouraging and directly supporting the development of the capacity of their neighboring communities to organize their resources, human and physical, so that they can negotiate their position in the social structure. The universities should pay communities for their knowledge and expertise, rather than merely use them as a research and training environment for future social scientists.

Reservations have been expressed about the utilization of communities as laboratories for action research, a relationship which tends to result in publication and advancement in the academy, but little or no basic change in the beset community. Consideration should be given to the sharing of royalties with the communities under investigation along with the appropriate acknowledgment of their contribution. If no institutional structures for these purposes exist, appropriate ones can be created to share in such rewards.

4. The university should establish interdisciplinary centers for the study of social phenomena that will provide the environment and opportunity for faculty from different disciplines to focus on major issues. I am not sure as to the degree of success attained by universities that have adopted this approach. I do know that the reward system of the university is not designed to encourage team-oriented social research. The construction of theoretical models that might aid us in our understanding of social phenomena demands inputs from various disciplines. Interdisciplinary centers should be organized so that faculty and students from various departments can participate on an as-needed basis, depending on the area of inquiry. Such interdisciplinary activity should include participation from the community through individuals who can contribute to the formulation and understanding of the problems at hand.

Support for this approach must come not only from the university as an institution, but from the faculty. The efforts required to deal with problems that go beyond the boundaries of individual disciplines require a strong shared commitment by the relevant faculty that transcends their normal individualistic tendencies. Out of this process could develop a unity of forces—community, students, and faculty—that through a closer linkage with one another would bring a new strength to bear on present problems of both university and community.

5. *The state and municipal universities should adopt the open enrolment plan of the City University of New York in order to provide a college educational opportunity to all high school graduates and create the environment for a culturally pluralistic educational experience.* Culturally pluralistic approaches to education do not automatically occur because poor ethnic minority high school graduates attend college. It is clear that there also must be administrative and educational creativity that takes advantage of the presence of such students. However, it is also necessary to consciously create the conditions under which such creativity can bear fruit. Open enrolment provides the conditions and the opportunity.

Of course there have been some states that have had open enrolment in their universities. Ohio State University has had open admissions for over fifty years. The University of California at Berkeley has been assuring admission for over a decade. In California there is a complete network of educational facilities and opportunities. A high school graduate has access to a community college, a state college, or a university center.

New York City is still unique. The City University of New York's retention rate for freshmen is better than pre-open enrolment days—88.2 percent of the freshmen have become sophomores.[7] The City University is not spreading its new enrolees throughout a state system but a municipal system. The enrolees are from and locked into an urban environment. The nature of their educational experience will determine, to a significant degree, the quality and relevance of the City University of New York to that urban scene.

[7] *New York Times*, March 26, 1971.

6. *The community must organize and structure itself so that its publics can make a positive contribution to the community's dialogue with educational institutions concerning goals and objectives.* There are parent organizations in our primary and secondary school systems that are deeply concerned about the educational direction of their schools. There are often civic groups in the field of child care and education that also express themselves on educational issues. At the graduate and undergraduate level there are professional associations and alumni associations, along with the business community, that from time to time effectively influence education in general and more often specific colleges and universities. We are all aware of the growing influence of organized labor in the field of education. Often these publics vary in their point of view on specific issues in the area of education.

It is precisely because a variety of publics have a vested interest in, and exert influence on, educational policies that the community must concern itself with the entire range of activities of the university. It is the community's concern with the overall policies of this institution with enormous resources at its control that will ultimately make it possible for the community to affect the educational policy of the university. The community must organize itself in a way in which it can communicate with the university on other than educational issues. It must also define for itself the strategies of engagement to insure effective results.

The educational establishments often indicate they are in trouble whether they do or do not follow the recommendations of the various groups that petition them to modify or adjust their directions. Of course this *is* often the case. But much of the hostility is a result of years of frustration relating to concerns about the purposes and the products of the various educational systems. There is also an absence of defined organizational and procedural strategies by the community and the educational institutions.

Remembering that particularly at the higher educational institutional level, concerns about their educational policies and procedures transcend the community where they physically reside, communities must enter into discussions with their educational institutions to determine the best way in which they can each contribute to a mutually beneficial relationship.

7. *Communities ought to consider the feasibility of developing information systems that will facilitate their interaction with educational and other institutions within their community.* A critical problem that communities always face is their being perceived continually as the object of activities of the various institutions that affect the lifestyles of their

residents. There often is a general sense of always reacting to changes rather than participating as an active agent in the process that leads to the determination that such changes ought to occur. Communities simply are not organized to relate, in a systematic way, to the many agencies that have responsibility to function in their interest.

One possible way to begin to come to grips with the problem is to develop the kind of information system that maximizes the possibility that those institutions will increase their use of the community as a resource rather than only as an object of activity. The correctly organized community may be the best source of information about population trends and residential patterns that is necessary for proper planning of school facilities and faculty levels. Graduate and undergraduate students could utilize such information centers as a source of current information in relation to their required course work. The communities would be in a position to enter into contract with educational and other institutions for the provision of appropriate information that would enable them to be more responsive to the needs of the community. The residents themselves, through their various participating organizations, would be able to secure updated information about the communities' needs so that they could present their positions on community issues more convincingly. The data base for the information system would be inclusive of questions whose answers would facilitate better planning by those agencies and institutions as well as questions that might make it possible to update the census continually.

Of course such an approach raises all kinds of questions, including the one of privacy. I think that one of the current problems is that agencies and institutions have information about residents of a community that the people in a community do not have. It is the uneven distribution or dissemination of such information that creates the major problem. If communities could devise the appropriate organizational structure for the gathering and analyzing of data and the dissemination of information, safeguards could be devised that would ensure that the source of the input could update the master files and could determine the form in which the information was disseminated. Such a system must evolve in an institutional setting recognized by the community as representing their interest.

Inherent in the problem of cultural discrimination is the notion that certain groups of people are inferior and have nothing of substance to contribute to our society or its institutions. The development of adequate information systems at the community institutional level allows for the nurturing of the notion that people, regardless of their cultural background, can contribute to the dialectics of democracy.

8. Communities should negotiate the inclusion of their existence and activity as an essential part of the educational process. It is easy to think of our educational institutions on any level as impersonal brick and mortar structures within which certain activity occurs. Education is a process of teaching and acquiring knowledge for living in our social system. The process is not simply a function of brick and mortar. Many communities have performed significant roles in enhancing the educational process. As the activities of communities are organized in ways that are perceived to be meaningful and substantive by the communities and our educational institutions alike, the communities will have greater influence on what is studied about them and the policies that affect them. Whether it is clearly understood or not, we are all living in a situation in which our communities provide a laboratory for learning that is hard to duplicate in the classroom environment. If this is true, the community and the university can work together to devise a peer relationship situation in which both can learn from each other. The institutional politics of such a process demands that our educational systems acknowledge that there is something to learn from an organized community. I might add that such an understanding and subsequent relationship might improve the effectiveness of the development of urban simulation models as a way of understanding urban centers and their communities.

9. Schools of education must lead the fight for sound management training for those individuals who desire administrative positions within the school system. The major responsibility of a good administrator or manager is to define the objectives of the institution that is his responsibility and develop a goal-setting procedure to ensure that the objectives are met.

Sound culturally pluralistic approaches to education cannot occur in a school or school system that does not have sound management design. You can always find individual teachers who attempt and often become successful at creating the right classroom environment for learning. I am not, however, discussing how one survives in the system. I am stressing the need for administrative and management supports to ensure success.

The problem for many large school systems is that major management decisions and responsibilities are vested centrally. Many of us have the notion that we would like the principal of the school to be a "headmaster"—really the master teacher. The fact is that in most systems he has no time to perform that role. He is managing a $2-3 million facility, with responsibilities to the community and to his teaching staff that transcend educational matters.

Schools of education must participate in the dialogue that comes to grips with the problems of and solutions to educational management. There is still debate as to which functions in the educational system ought to be centralized and which ought to be decentralized. But more serious than that is the fact that people performing administrative functions often do so without training. In many school systems, pedagogical experience, frequently in unrelated fields, is accepted as qualification for such management functions as planning, evaluation, accounting, and budget analysis. Supervisory experience alone does not make a teacher a manager.

10. Schools of education must support the development of programs that allow teachers to progress professionally and monetarily while functioning in a teaching environment. Part of the problem relating to quality education is that the growth options for teachers narrow considerably. If a teacher does not move into the administrative "line of succession," it is difficult, if not impossible, for that individual to move up the professional ladder. The universities now recognize this problem. More and more special chairs are created that in many cases reward individuals who have made significant contributions in their fields. Special titles are often conferred on professors that allow them to secure additional income from the university beyond the scale that is normative for the position. These are all attempts, in most cases, to single out the best of faculty. The selected ones may never be the chairman of a department, or a dean, or the president of the university. They can, however, achieve a monetary and status position that is recognized as equally important.

It is time for some application of this procedure to occur in the primary and secondary school systems. To achieve such a system will require the leadership of the segment of the educational establishment that is involved in teacher training. Not every teacher wants to be or can best make his educational contribution as a manager or administrator. Institutions of teacher training must initiate an approach to school systems with the objective of developing an avenue of professional growth for those individuals who are desirous of remaining in the classroom.

11. Schools of education must expand the opportunities for their students to acquire teaching skills in a culturally pluralistic environment. The teaching degree does not state that there are limitations on the competency of the new teacher in the areas of teaching middle- or lower-class youth or students of certain cultural backgrounds. There is an assumption that the teacher is always competent and that failure is a student responsibility. This approach simply heightens communication problems between the student and the teacher. Students have contributions to make to the educational process. The teacher can also acquire knowledge from his students.

In order to enhance such an opportunity the schools of education should expose their students to teaching and living in a pluralistic environment. An opportunity of this nature is being provided by Stonybrook College of the State University of New York. Their Urban In-Residence Teacher Education Program provides for the taking of three years of liberal arts courses and the earning of the fourth-year total educational sequence by living in the inner city community with families. The students work in the school from 9:00 a.m. to 3:00 p.m; from 3:00 p.m. to 5:00 p.m. they do work in the community. They also utilize their evenings in community-affiliated work.

This experience enables the teacher to understand to a greater degree the environment and the people inclusive of the children that will be in attendance in the schools. A significant ingredient in the program was the community's contribution to its design. In addition, fiscal resources that normally would have been allocated for dormitory residence are paid to the host families for room and board. The families are an educational resource and an extension of the university.

12. The school system must evolve an administrative structure that unites the principal, teacher, curriculum, and student in the culturally pluralistic experience. We know that public educational philosophy developed exclusive of the participation of Blacks and other minorities in the social order. We also know that three of the major functions of education—cultural transmission, the development of self-identity in the individual, and socialization—were advanced in the school but were sustained and continued primarily in the home, in the religious community, in the polity, and through participation in the economy. The minority child could attend only certain schools, the family has had generations of slavery that was destructive to home life, their religious communities were segregated, and they could not equally participate in the polity and the economy. It is no wonder that quality education was unachievable.

For the culturally pluralistic experience to occur in our schools, the process must be understood in organic terms. The administrative environment must be set and the atmosphere created that encourages the participants in the educational process to share equally what each has to contribute to that process.

It will be of no avail if the schools of education produce graduates that are prepared to be a part of such an organic whole only to find that no such notion exists in the schools to which they are assigned.

13. The principal should encourage and support educational changes that permit the teacher to relate to the student as an individual. The difference between teaching and many other occupations is that education purports to be an objective process and is subjectively administered. Statements by principals that "they are all the same to me," are meant to deny discriminatory inclinations, and to imply that they are treating all students equally. In confusing similarity of treatment with equality, they miss a crucial point: There are real differences in customs, values, and beliefs which have reality and essence in the students' subculture. If the goal is to treat students with equality, then these differences among students, ethnic and otherwise, must be recognized, and the students' specific needs must be understood within the context of tradition and cultural experience. Equality of response is the important thing, and not similarity of treatment or of educational services.

There is new educational technology, some occuring in the New York City school system on a small scale, that permits greater individuality. Let me briefly tell you about a program in operation at four junior high schools in a local district. This program lets the students move at their own rate of comprehension and keeps the teacher informed of the specific needs of every child in his classes on a daily basis. Essentially, it is a program of computer-managed instruction. There is no direct interchange between the computer and the child. The teacher does all the teaching, relieved, incidentally, of many irksome clerical tasks such as attendance taking which are simply taken care of as by-products of the program. Programmed instruction material is used, and, on the basis of daily quizzes, the child is directed to what he needs next. In these junior high schools, the teacher has five classes a day of about thirty pupils each and could not keep track of the needs of his students without assistance.

The computer monitors the child's work, feeding back information on his status, analyzing his progress and needs, and analyzing the material in order to determine whether it is presenting its information in a usable way. Self-review is written into the program. If too many of the children are not getting the right answers on a particular quiz or question, then there is something wrong with the way the material is being presented. The information or particular question or quizzes are then reformulated.

The teacher is the key element in the program, and he understands that the program is a servant and not a replacement. The teachers from the four schools involved had written up the lesson materials and devised the quizzes in conjunction with the designer of the program on a grant from the State Education Department. The program got under way in November, 1970 after two years of preliminary work.

The personnel involved feel they are seeing positive results already. Teacher accountability is inherent in the program, measured by the teachers' responses to the students' needs as reported on the daily computer print-outs. The principal and his staff receive copies of these reports and this increases their management capability. As a result teachers are spending the major part of the day in teaching. Morale is very high, pupils are learning, parents are pleased.

14. The teacher must create and maintain a classroom environment that supports objectivity and freedom of inquiry. Rational, objective, and scientific thinking about each other on the part of students can reduce the defensive impulses toward stereotypic thinking and the closed mind. Behavior which was previously guided by superstition, lack of knowledge, and fear must be guided by access to correct information, understanding, and intelligent discrimination. This provides the foundation for the student's perception of the world and the people in it.

The teacher must accept a positive recognition of human differences. He must not be intimidated from doing this by his own revulsion from the sad tradition of negative use that has been made of these differences. Then, the teacher's recognition and discussion of human differences can open a whole new world of learning for teachers and students alike. Such discussions will provide a basis for wise decision-making in the student's estimate of himself, his classmates, and the people of diverse cultural backgrounds whom he will encounter in the adult world.

The teacher is a manager of the classroom environment and the interaction between him and his students is fundamentally a sociopsychological process. The willingness to include the student as a part of the organic whole is essential to the success of the teacher's endeavors.

We know that all the skills needed to subsist in our society are acquired after birth and that along with achievement levels and scholarship the ability to accept the equal essence of man, cultural differences, and self images unbiased by prejudice and misconceptions of self worth are all intrinsic to good education. Man must learn to live with others in dignity before his capabilities can be fully manifested. Education can and must provide tools, techniques, and opportunities through which such existence can be assured.

8

AN IMPEDIMENT TO CULTURAL PLURALISM: CULTURALLY DEFICIENT EDUCATORS ATTEMPTING TO TEACH CULTURALLY DIFFERENT CHILDREN

JOHN ARAGON

For some time now we have copped out on serious consideration of the concept of cultural pluralism by using astute and even intelligent-sounding rhetoric to avoid assuming any responsibility for it. We have been quite effective in shifting the responsibility for the recognition of cultural pluralism from the professional to the client. This, when we have chosen to recognize its existence at all. More commonly, however, we have refused to recognize that cultural pluralism exists, or even that it should. There are cases where educators (the term educator here is used in its broadest context), ranging all the way from professors of the liberal arts and education, school administrators, and up to primary teachers, have discounted pluralism by ascribing to culturally different clients (students) all kinds of demeaning terms. We are all familiar with these terms: culturally deficient, culturally disadvantaged, culturally deprived, and in extreme cases even culturally depraved.

In essence, we have absolved ourselves by stating that the problem belongs to the learner and that it is his responsibility to overcome it; that it is his responsibility to adjust; that it is his responsibility to learn about me; that it is his responsibility to become an American. These are the kinds of statements which can only be called astute rationalizations to avoid what the real issue is.

The true impediment to cultural pluralism is that we have had culturally deficient educators attempting to teach culturally different children. The reader may find this observation rather difficult to accept. He may feel that he has always been receptive to cultural pluralism, that he has always had respect for the culture of others.

This paper does not wish to take issue with what the reader feels; rather, it would like to direct itself to what we, each of us, have done, or better still what each of us has not done.

If we really have been accepting our cultural differences then why haven't we succeeded in producing a pluralistic society? The answer is rather obvious. Our intentions have been good. We really have been, and are, accepting them; we really believe in the dignity of man and we respect his differences. In essence we are all good guys. Granted that to one degree or another the preceding statements are all true in one way or another.

The answer is then painfully obvious; it has to be one of two things. Either we are all a bunch of hypocrites and we choose to believe good things about ourselves, when in reality we don't practice them, or we are culturally deficient in acknowledging those cultural differences that our clients bring to us.

I choose to believe the latter. Our sins are sins of omission rather than commission. We can't teach within a context where cultural differences are extant if we don't know what the cultural differences are. Therein lies our dilemma. We can't teach what we don't know. The deficiency thus is in the professional, not the client.

Before serious consideration can be given to the concept of cultural pluralism we must define what culture is. The writer's definition of culture will begin with what culture is not. Culture is not a word followed by disadvantaged, defective, or deprived. Nor is it the culture of poverty. All too often we have chosen to confuse the culture of poverty with true cultural differences. Cultural differences cannot be ascribed to the disadvantages, however real and painful, of socioeconomic class. This is what the culture of poverty alludes to. Culture, by our definition, is not used in the same context as the word "culture" in the "culture of poverty." Culture of poverty refers to all people who are economically deprived and has little to do with ethnicity or true and identifiable cultural traits. People in the culture of poverty are poor; they are poor first and then they are WASPs from West Virginia; they are poor first and then Black; they are poor first and then they are Mexicans. Thus, the kind of cultural pluralism of which we are speaking has little to do with the culture of poverty.

What, then, is culture in the context of cultural pluralism? The writer, who currently directs the Cultural Awareness Center at the University of New Mexico, and members of the staff surveyed the literature for a meaningful definition of culture and discovered great variance in what people tend to define as culture. Educators in the public schools, we discovered, tend to think of culture as the culture of poverty at worst, or at best, think that culture means an appreciation of the fine arts. Anthropologists tend to think of culture as being the sum total of man's acquired knowledge. This latter definition is quite good but not quite specific enough for our use. Sociologists have written volumes on culture. They, too, have many good definitions.

However, none of them were viable enough for our purpose; thus, the writer has derived his own definition of culture and is prepared to defend the proposition that culture is composed of at least five vital components. He believes that should one go anywhere in the world and find a group of people who are homogenous in the following five areas one can safely say, "I think we have a culture here." If these people all verbalize the same sounds in order to communicate or if they speak the same *language*, we think we have one component of culture. If these people all nurture their bodies with basically the same kinds of foods or if they have a common *diet*, we think we have a second component of culture. If these people all adorn or protect their bodies with the same kinds of dress or *costuming*, we think we have a third component of culture. If these people relate to one another in a predictable fashion, if the relationship between mother and daughter, grandfather and grandson, uncle and niece follows a normative pattern, or if they have common *social patterns*, we think we have a fourth component of culture. And if these people have a common set of values and beliefs, or *ethics*, we think we have a fifth component of culture.

Thus the writer believes that culture, in the context of cultural pluralism, would include commonality among individuals within any given group in: (1) language, (2) diet, (3) costuming, (4) social patterns, and (5) ethics.

If the reader will accept this as one definition of culture, then the question is, "how can professionals who do not have these five components in common with their clients subscribe to and teach toward the concept of cultural pluralism?" It isn't easy. However, no one has ever claimed that education is easy or simple.

The preceding sections have established a rationale and a philosophical basis for the succeeding sections. The succeeding sections will attempt to detail a program for the realization of the objectives of educational pluralism.

We have already claimed that the deficiencies are to be found in the educator and not in the client. An attempt will now be made to suggest a procedure through which these claimed deficiencies may be overcome.

The first section will detail a program to (1) meet the needs, (2) acquire better understandings, and (3) develop strategies for dealing with the education of the culturally different child. These sections will detail the same things as they affect personnel relevant to the school program.

All sections will be placed in the context of "The Esperanza Model." This was developed by a number of people, and those who contributed to the model in various stages of its development include Drs. Thomas Arciniega, John Aragon, Frank Angel, and Mari-Luci Ulibarri. Dr. Ulibarri used this model in her doctoral dissertation, "In-Service Teacher Education in a Tri-Ethnic Community: A Participant-Observer Study."[1]

The model was actually applied in a school district in New Mexico during the academic years 1968-1969 and 1969-1970 where it met with the desired results. Dr. Ulibarri stated that the purpose of the study was to observe and record processes during the implementation of an in-service education model used to change the behavior of teachers, administrators, and school board members in order to better meet the needs of a tri-ethnic community.

Dr. Ulibarri further states that the multilevel approach, in itself novel, was part of an overall new attack on the problems faced by the school district. She adds that previous programs certainly had been moving in the right direction, but by no means were sufficient to meet the problems because, fundamentally, they were attacking only one facet of a multifaceted problem. The biggest weaknesses of the programs were that they were not inclusive of the critical factors of the issue.

The Model

This model assumes that the people using it are desirous of enriching the educational program (a monocultural one) to provide relevant and self-actualizing experiences for the culturally different child, but also to enrich the life of the Anglo child as well.

[1] Unpublished Ph.D. dissertation, University of New Mexico, May, 1970.

The Teacher

Phase I: Awareness

Phase I deals with awareness. It is presumed that school authorities must first be made aware that different cultures are in evidence all over the nation, but in particular in the Spanish-speaking Southwest.

SECTION 1: SELF NEEDS

In Section 1 of Phase I the school staff participating in the application of the model are divided into groups of ten to twelve persons. These groups should be representative of all the participants. The groups meet eight or ten times, with each session lasting from four to six hours. A skilled discussion leader is indispensable to guarantee that the individuals in the group cover all the pertinent and necessary issues that will enable them to meet their individual self needs, and to guarantee fair play as the groups begin to speak about insecurities, apathy, complacency, narrow commitment, tradition, personal prejudices, and other behavioral traits which must be candidly re-examined before an individual can be predisposed to effectively begin to accept the concept of cultural pluralism in his school job. Once the participants have eradicated all of the factors which tend to impede each individual's openness, and once the participants have discovered and understood their self needs, the groups are dissolved. The participants then move into Section 2 of Phase I. This usually occurs a month after the initial application of the model. Readings may and should be assigned and provided to the participants.

SECTION 2: CULTURAL DIVERSITY

Section 2 will have the entire group of participants meeting together again. For this section the school district must provide speakers who are knowledgeable about the cultural groups represented in the school district. It is here that one taps the resources in arts and sciences. Lecturers in sociology, anthropology, and history are invited to participate. Lectures are presented to the entire group and then the participants are assigned to smaller groups to discuss the lectures. The lecturer or consultants are available to each group for questions, elaborations, or clarifications. These lecture sessions will vary in number depending on how many different cultures are represented in the community. If the community is limited to Mexican and Anglo Americans, four to six lectures for each group may suffice. If the community has more cultural groups than these two, the time and lectures will have to be expanded.

On a national and regional level people such as Julian Zamora of Notre

Dame; Horacio Ulibarri of Southern Methodist University; and Armando Rodriguez of the Office of Mexican-American Affairs, Washington, D.C., are available or can recommend knowledgeable people. Many resources, however, are available within the school district or very close by if one will only look for them.

At the conclusion of this activity the group should have an adequate understanding of its community as well as what each culture represents.

SECTION 3: CULTURAL CONFLICTS

Section 3 of Phase I will be conducted the same as the previous section, perhaps even using the same consultants. However, the focal point here will be on the identification of where the cultures may conflict. Consultants will have to be acquired to speak on conflicts between and among perceptions stemming from diverse cultural practices. Examples covered might include: Do they view, in different ways, things such as the school, the family, language, and ethics? Once having identified these, the participants are now ready to proceed to the next step.

SECTION 4: IMPLICATIONS OF CULTURAL CONFLICT

Section 4 of Phase I will follow the same procedures as the preceding sections, except that here the focus will be on where the cultures conflict, rather than on identifying the differences between the cultures.

At this point the "Awareness" phase is completed. The participant has identified his own needs, he has been provided with content on cultures, and he has participated in identifying the areas where cultures conflict and the implications these have in teaching.

Phase II: Application of Awareness

SECTION 1: CLASSIFICATION OF TEACHER'S STYLE

In this section the teacher's style is identified. It is analyzed in terms of the kind of educational philosophy to which that style best lends itself. The teacher is thus helped to analyze himself/herself and to identify the school of learning theory to which he/she belongs. Flander's Inter-action Analysis or a microlab are two of many techniques which may be used.

SECTION 2: CRITICAL LOOK AT THE TOTAL SCHOOL
PROGRAM OF HIS/HER SCHOOL DISTRICT

At this point teachers are divided into groups that are representative of the entire school system. Each group should include administrators and teachers of various grade levels, so that a total analysis of that entire district's program can be made, using resources from all levels of the school. The teachers should now have a clear understanding of the entire scope and sequence of the program in their particular school.

The sole purpose of this section is to make available to the entire personnel of the school district the accumulated knowledge of the teacher and administrator in the areas of culture, cultural diversity, cultural conflict, and the teacher's teaching style, and known learning theories.

The school district's own program is critically analyzed in terms of the staff's acquired knowledge in the previous sections.

The staff is broken down into groups representative of all school levels. Each group should view the school district in its entirety, then broken down into groups of areas of specialization. These areas are criticized by those people who are directly involved in that portion of the educational program.

A list of strengths and shortcomings is now written by each group's area of specialization. The strengths are retained and activity begins toward correcting the shortcomings.

SECTION 3: SURVEY OF THE COMMUNITY OF
AVAILABLE HUMAN AND MATERIAL RESOURCES

The function of this section is to correct the identified weaknesses in the curriculum.

The teachers are divided into teams of two or three people of common academic and curricular interests. These people identify how they can survey the community to acquire the information of relevant and existing human and material resources. Then they go out into the community and do it.

Their findings are now developed into teaching units to complement and enrich their respective subject matter areas.

At this point the school district has a large volume of community and culturally relevant resources both human and material.

Phase III: Logistics for Implementation

This phase is self explanatory. It merely encompasses the traditional steps taken by school people prior to adoption by the school board. Each school administrator has taken countless courses on how to work with curricular modifications, in-service programs, school-community projects, and how to make and acquire support for recommendations.

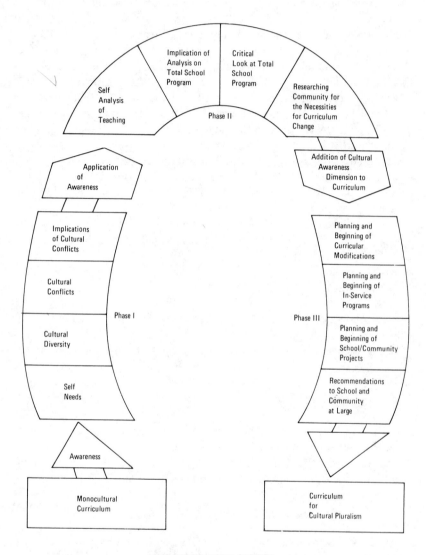

THE ESPERANZA MODEL:
CULTURAL AWARENESS AND APPLICATION TO CURRICULUM

9

THE DEVELOPMENT OF TEACHING MATERIALS
FOR CULTURAL PLURALISM:
THE PROBLEM OF LITERACY

MALCOLM P. DOUGLASS

There can be no argument that the central and abiding issue in teaching and learning today, at least in the United States, is that of finding ways of helping all children achieve adequate levels of literacy. Strangely, in a country endowed with great wealth and boundless faith in the powers of science and technology in bringing about solutions to any problem to which we might wish to give our attention and energy, Americans find themselves with the highest levels of reading disability in the world, at least among those nations whose national goals include universal literacy. Compounding the nationwide problem is the endemic and exceedingly high incidence of reading disability among our major ethnic and racial minorities. While it is presently conceded that about 25 percent of the American population at large "has significant reading deficiencies,"[1] it must be remembered that figure skyrockets to 80 to 90 percent in a very large proportion of the urban and rural slums and ghettos.

This reading problem is not new. Its existence and its apparent severity in society at large have received widespread notice for at least a century or

[1] James E. Allen, Jr., "The Right to Read—Target for the 70's," Address by the . U.S. Commissioner of Education before the 1969 Annual Convention of the National Association of State Boards of Education, Los Angeles, California, September 23, 1969.

more, However, a previously ignored and most severe dimension of it is now being recognized in a special context. That is the particular and vexing question of finding, quickly, a solution to the extraordinarily high incidence of reading and writing deficiency existing among people who have been denied entry into the mainstream of American life for racial, ethnic, or economic reasons, or for some combination of these.

The matter is now rapidly escalating in importance partly because we are living in an age when it is no longer admirable or acceptable to find one's way in life by dropping out of school and "going to work." Indeed, today a high school education provides a barely acceptable minimum if one is to gain that kind of employment sufficiently remunerative to provide a fair share of the material rewards brought about by the recent and spectacular advances in science and technology.[2] And, given the standards we hold as a nation, especially with regard to our professed and oft-quoted belief in equal opportunities for all, it is little wonder that major segments of our population, now growing rapidly in awareness of the nature, extent, and degree of those inequities that have prevented them from sharing equally in the material and other benefits of American life in the 1970's, see their situation not only as intolerable but also as no longer endurable.

As leading members of those minority populations being denied access to the "good life" analyze the situation, the highest priority is being placed upon solving the problem of literacy. The grave reading and writing deficiencies are considered to be the major stumbling blocks in gaining access to "mainstream America," and it is consequently believed that the key to their problem is to be found in developing ways of teaching that will eliminate the extraordinarily high failure rate which, without any question whatsoever, characterizes the school experience of minority children.

Because of this very grave concern on the part of the leaders of minority groups where literacy problems are endemic, I shall concentrate my remarks here to the development of teaching materials that relate to finding relief for this very serious problem. In its totality, the question of teaching materials is obviously a very broad one. This is especially the case in the United States, which enjoys the most bountiful supply, in almost infinite variation, of any country in the world. But the presence of these materials obviously has not significantly changed the patterns of reading

[2] Charles E. Silberman, *Crisis in the Classroom* (New York: Random House, 1970), pp. 18-20.

deficiencies either in the population at large or in those circumstances of special concern for those of us attending this conference. Hence, I feel that as we look at the nature of those materials, we must not only make some educated guesses as to why they have not provided the always hoped for panacea in solving what we are currently calling "the reading problem." At the same time, we ought to look beyond what we usually think about when someone mentions "teaching materials." Clearly, the question of teaching materials must be considered in that broader light if anything fruitful is to come from this discussion.

Teaching Materials and the Marketplace

First, however, one cannot understand adequately the current educational scene as it relates to reading instruction without reflecting upon the manner in which the vast and unmatched reservoir of teaching materials available in the United States has come into existence (and the concomitant faith that has developed regarding their place in the classroom as well as their power in solving the reading problem). Of prime importance in any consideration of reading instruction is the role of the marketplace in the development of those materials. In the United States, unlike any other country in the world, reading is truly Big Business. That market, after all, consists of some sixty or seventy million school-age children (more people overall than populate the British Isles); there are, as well, over two million teachers. With such a vast market, fortunes can, have, and will continue to be made—true fortunes in the image of the great American dream. It is not surprising that the American marketplace in reading is as fiercely competitive as it is rewarding.

In the logical course of events, one would hope and expect that these products of the marketplace would reflect the findings of basic research. After all, publishers long have allied themselves with professional educators and teachers in determining what might be the nature of their product. At the same time, no educational concern has been subjected to more "research" than has reading itself. The strange fact of the matter, however, is that little of that research has been truly basic in character. The product itself, rarely field tested in any serious way, has emerged as a result of the expert's interpretation of research directed primarily to questions dealing with the relative effectiveness of different already-existing approaches, after carefully tuning into what it was believed teachers either already wanted or could be "sold" into thinking would be effective in classroom use. One result has been that the large number of materials available are remarkably similar. Designed to reach the widest possible market, they do not meet the special needs of groups within the society. Rather, they reflect the dominant middle-core of society.

I have noted that only recently has basic research in reading been undertaken. By basic research I refer to the study of questions surrounding the most fundamental one of all: What is reading and how is it related to the other forms of human language? Strange as it may seem, the kind of research in reading and language learning generally that would give us clues about the effects of present instruction as well as information about how language is acquired has begun to be conducted in earnest only during the past eight or ten years. Additionally, that research comes to us not so much from the field of education, as from sociology, medicine, linguistics, anthropology, and several other of the social and humanistic fields of inquiry. Because previous research has been based on such a narrow conception of reading behavior, most of us have assumed that everyone agrees as to what reading is and how it ought to be taught, considering it to be something capable of being defined narrowly and specifically. Generally the view is that reading is a subject in the school curriculum, that reading itself is a skill which is learned by being exposed to said subject matter. Finally, the subject matter of reading is what is contained in the various reading textbooks. Only recently have data begun to become available which indicate that reading is no more a "subject" that can be taught and learned like arithmetic or geography than is speaking a subject or skill that is learned in a similar fashion.

Nonetheless, the subject-matter point of view in reading has dominated the preparation of textbooks, and it continues to do so. However, I believe this position will be displaced before long as inquiry into the nature of the reading process is expanded upon. For in these more basic studies it is becoming increasingly apparent that reading is a much more complex behavior than heretofore imagined.[3] Its emergence, or its failure to develop, derives from a host of interactions, many if not most being of an extremely subtle nature. The inevitable conclusion is that reading behavior is not evoked primarily through teaching the surface or obvious characteristics of the phonological system as it is represented in its printed or written form. Rather, it appears to emerge more as a consequence of the

---

[3] For example, see: Harry Levin and Joanna P. Williams, eds., *Basic Studies on Reading* (New York: Basic Books, 1970), p. ix.

desire to generate ideas and to get in some kind of communication with the ideas of others.

A parallel conclusion is that there is no valid reason why anyone with sufficient intelligence to function as an independent human being should fail to learn to read and write the oral language he already knows so well. It should be obvious, of course, that the quality of that reading and writing will reflect the competence of the individual to think and reason, just as experience provides the base for determining what kind of reading will engage his interests. However, the ability itself resides in every individual; when we come across deficiencies we can only conclude that there are other factors at work to which we must give our attention so that the capacity for reading and language use in general will emerge.

Put another way, the reading problem is not uniquely related to one's racial or ethnic origins. It is, rather, related to those social, economic, and cultural conditions surrounding life as it is lived in the community and in the school.

I have suggested, then, that materials alone are not enough. Yet, it is obvious that some kind of teaching material must be employed; and it is equally clear that we are in many ways bound by what is already available. I have suggested, as well, that our current situation is strongly under the spell of the marketplace; that the books, supplementary texts, workbooks, and all the rest of the vast array of teaching materials have become available primarily as a consequence of what publishers have believed they could sell. That these materials have been designed for a national market is also well known. Regional differences and special problems, if any, of certain racial and ethnic minorities have until very recently, at least, been overlooked.

The Current Scene

The common solution proposed in the United States for correcting the reading problem is intensification and extension of instruction, plus employment of more reading materials. (Extension of instruction into the upper grades and the proliferation of teaching materials themselves are some of the more obvious responses to this conception.) The assumption is being made, as well, that the teaching materials available are essentially sound; thus the problem is not within the materials themselves but within the manner in which they are used. If a little use produces (or appears to produce) "x" result, the reasoning goes, greater usage will result in "x^2"

achievement. This argument is a rather universal one; it is also one that leaders in the Mexican-American and Black communities are attracted to. It is also one to which I cannot subscribe, and in the discussion following, I trust my reasons will become clear and potentially useful in pointing to alternatives.

However, I do believe it is not only possible but necessary to use currently available materials, despite the grave shortcomings to which they are subject. To point up these possibilities, it is necessary for me to state my case with regard to the materials themselves and to the kind of program I am convinced we must have if any real progress in the teaching of reading is to be made. I should first like to describe the current scene in some detail, moving from there to criteria for developing a sound reading program capable of utilizing, at least to a certain degree, that which is already available to us in the way of teaching materials themselves.

Today, every textbook of which I have any knowledge has been written with the presumption that the teacher will organize pupils into at least three groups according to their achievement, i.e., their apparent ability to work successfully with the subject matter the stories are designed to teach. Such practices persist and even expand in the face of a growing body of data that not only do not support them but show that such groupings have negative effects upon achievement. And now, research is beginning to present us with some fascinating data on the self-fulfilling prophecy, not only with regard to achievement itself, but with respect to attitudes and feelings of self-worth.[4]

The single most compelling argument for achievement grouping remains the convenience and attitude of the teacher. However, in the face of the other data on achievement, attitudes, and behavior in general, that argument can no longer be accepted as valid. The long-term result of such grouping practices in the elementary school can be seen in the complexly tracked secondary school where overt behavior problems now emerge especially among those whose school lives have been spent in "the bottom group," a place that has for so many years carried the implicit if not so explicit message of their unworthiness as human beings.

I cannot state too strongly my aversion to achievement grouping in reading. The practice cannot be supported for numerous reasons, but among the most cogent is the impossibility of approximating similar achievement levels. The "fact" of achievement grouping is therefore only a

[4] See, for example: Miriam L. Goldberg, et al., *The Effects of Ability Grouping* (New York: Teachers College, Columbia University, 1966); J. W. B. Douglas, *The Home and the School* (London: MacGibbon & Kee, 1964).

myth. But even more important, the social stigma associated with identifying elite groups within a class is antidemocratic. It constitutes a peculiarly virulent but largely unrecognized form of segregation.[5] There is also insufficient evidence that such grouping in and of itself enhances learning. Most data show either no superiority for grouping or that it is deleterious. If my only choice were between total group instruction in reading and achievement grouping, I would select the former. However, there is another alternative: individualization of instruction, a procedure to which I shall return shortly.

The second development in methods of teaching relates to the amount of time devoted to teaching the subject of reading. We have expanded the amount of time devoted to instruction at the same time publishers have supplied us with an ever-increasing array of textbooks, workbooks, supplementary books, special kits, and the like. Under the presumption that more of the same is the answer, large numbers of school people seriously propose that the solution to the problem is to throw out virtually everything else and spend the entire school day on reading. Publishers cooperate by providing materials which, if followed explicitly, would accomplish just that. For an example of this trend, we can note that forty years ago one text per grade was optimal; within that text children "met up" with more different words but in a shorter period of time. And where entire textbooks of the late 1800's contained perhaps three or four pages of instructions to the teacher, one series popular today which included 561 words per average lesson in 1920 provided 2,000 in 1962![6]

Reading is much too subtle a process to respond to such heavy-handed techniques. First, because reading is an individual, highly personal form of behavior, it is difficult to understand why we would think that grouping children in a fashion that highlights inadequacies is a beneficial way to proceed—as is the case where achievement groups illuminate differences and make mistakes or errors more obvious, unimportant as they may seem to the adult. Second, extending instructional time to overcome deficiencies merely places children in failure situations for longer periods of time. Third, the logic remains to be proved in the deduction that those skills and abilities we observe in mature reading behavior can be taught directly. And fourth, the emphasis upon materials as the cure for reading problems, which is so attractive to those who would sell their own reading programs,

[5] Bruno Bettleheim, "Segregation: New Style," *School Review*, Vol. 66 (Autumn, 1958), pp. 251-272.

[6] Jeanne S. Chall, *Learning to Read: The Great Debate* (New York: McGraw-Hill, 1967), p. 257.

suggests that teachers are incapable themselves of evoking reading behavior without the authoritative voice of others (as represented in the detailed "how to teach" suggestions that permeate all instructional guides).

Teaching Materials and Individualizing Instruction

I believe the most important reform immediately available to us is in finding ways to individualize the teaching of reading, utilizing materials presently available. The most widely obtainable teaching material is obviously the reading textbook itself; consequently, any immediate improvements in the learning of reading are in large measure dependent upon its use. In the face of questions about the quality of such materials for use with children, and particularly as regards the issue of racism and other forms of prejudice, I nevertheless believe the overriding issue is whether or not we can use these textbooks to truly individualize reading programs for our boys and girls. I consider it a prime responsibility of the publishing houses and the professional educators who have worked toward the development of basal reader series to include in their suggestions to teachers the simple ways in which true individualization of instruction may be done. However, in the long run, I view this as a stopgap procedure; there are important major shifts in teaching that I would advocate in the search for more effective means of enhancing language development in general and reading in particular—and I shall comment upon these in due course.

Individualizing teaching with presently available materials is extremely easy to accomplish. Given the nature of the reading process, it is neither necessary nor desirable to attempt to teach all children a specific set of skills nor is it desirable nor necessary to teach several children the same thing at the same time. This is because the direct teaching of skills is an inefficient means of evoking them in a child's behavior, but more importantly, because children apprehend many skills quite on their own. Moreover, different children require help on specific skills at different times. If teaching can be arranged so that help is given at the time of need, the time of both teacher and child will be released for more important activities— ones that will focus on reading per se. Hence, our job is to find reading materials attractive to the child, which that child can read under the guidance of a teacher whose background and attitudes are compatible with the pupils in his class, one who provides assistance as needed according to each child's needs. It is a very simple proposition that is naturally attuned to the idiosyncratic nature of reading development. Such individualization with currently available materials is possible and attainable. Only leadership on the part of educators, school administrators, and the publishing industry is required to achieve the shift from group to individualized instruction.

Teaching Materials and Multi-Ethnic Needs

Within the question of the overall adequacy of present textual materials, particular issues have been raised concerning the appropriateness of such materials for certain racial and ethnic minorities. There no longer seems any doubt that the vast majority of commercial materials presently available represent a narrow "white world" in which actual representation of minority interests, if it exists at all, is almost exclusively mere tokenism. While we have suspected materials for all sorts of devious reasons, more objective studies are now coming to our attention.[7] For example in a recent study of readers purporting to be "multi-ethnic" in character, the researchers found:

First, what may appear on the basis of its cover and promotional literature to be a multi-ethnic first-grade reading book may, on closer inspection, contain few significant characters of ethnic background other than white Anglo-Saxon. Second, including other ethnic groups does not necessarily imply that the environmental setting of the stories is any different than that of the traditional, suburban-oriented series. Third, although multi-ethnic series are not generally characterized by stories in which the main activity ends in failure, some authors may have a tendency to emphasize lack of success to a greater extent in their multi-ethnic series than they do in their traditional first-grade reading books.[8]

The long-range effects of such materials on attitudes and upon the development of reading abilities is not known. My own guess is that the content of the stories is not as important in teaching attitudes as we have thought; anyone who can read at all critically will see through such materials and reject them, going on to better literature. If any factor is as critically important, it is the attitude of the teacher toward the child's

[7] Jules Henry, "Reading for What?" *Claremont Reading Conference, 28th Yearbook*, 1961, pp. 19-35.
[8] Gaston E. Blom et al., "A Motivational Content Analysis of Children's Primers," in Levin and Williams, op. cit., Chapter 12, p. 200.

language and the school's capability for reflecting the interests of the parents it serves. Nonetheless, such materials are naturally suspect and the insensitivity of those who write and publish them is a matter apparently requiring concerted action if significant changes are to be achieved in the near future.

Another important question centers around the matter of the need for special materials, particularly with regard for readers written in the Black dialect and books prepared in Spanish for Mexican-American youngsters. Virtually no attention has been directed toward the language problems of the American Indian in this dimension.

In the case of the Black dialect, where the major differences from standard English are primarily grammatical rather than phonological or morphological, I concur with the growing opinion that special materials are not called for (with the possible exception of a few rather small uniquely special groups in the Deep South). The persuasive argument, in my view, centers around the fact that Negro children who speak a Black dialect appear to make their own substitutions or omissions in reading when there is conflict between their own language and that of the page as they progress in the business of "getting the hang" of the story. In effect, they will not detect a discrepancy between their own language and what is on the page, selecting that which fits, omitting other words, and changing still others to achieve the degree of congruence between oral speech and its written form necessary to meaning. This appears to happen *if* teaching does not require the child to repeat with complete accuracy each word in the text; in other words, where emphasis is upon meaning, upon the gist of the sentence or paragraph rather than upon the ability to identify individual words as a precondition of reading for meaning. That "if," I grant, is a large one. At the same time, if one were to argue that Black dialect should be encouraged as a second major language, a rationale for developing teaching materials in that dialect could easily be developed. However, this is not a position I would support.

The problem of the Mexican American in learning to read English is different from that of the Negro in at least two important respects. First, the syntax of the native language (to whatever degree it has developed) differs from English in substantive ways; hence, the expectation of what the next word might be, such an important ability in developing reading proficiency, is likely to be seriously impaired where the native Spanish speaker seeks to read English. Second, there are important pronunciation differences between English and Spanish. I believe we are a considerable distance from finding appropriate solutions to these problems. But at this juncture, I would submit that there are important regional questions to be considered. In other words, there is no one answer; successful responses will result when the teaching-learning plan varies from one area to another. Probably the easiest solution is obtainable in those areas of the country where the Mexican-American population lives in a world dominated exclusively by their native language and their culture. In such areas it makes sense to conduct the entire educational program in Spanish, at least until the age of ten or twelve, when the native language will not only be learned but there will have been opportunity for the school experience to enrich it and help it expand. We notice, for example, that children from Mexico entering schools in this country, where English is the language of instruction, at age ten or so appear to experience relatively little difficulty in acquiring English and in learning through that language. If schools in societies where the language is predominantly Spanish were conducted in that language, we might conceivably achieve a reasonably similar result. In other countries, where English is taught as a second language beginning around age eleven, we find other parallels potentially useful as models in achieving a solution to this particular problem.

However, it is the children who are exposed to both English and Spanish at earlier ages who appear to suffer the greatest handicaps in their overall language development. Where the child hears a mixture of Spanish and English from his earliest years, and lives in a very mixed community where cultural values in the home, school, and community are inconsistent or in conflict, we find the problem the most difficult to solve. Some bicultural/bilingual curriculums have been devised and are being tested out. It is my presumption that the most effective of these will involve the immediate community extensively in the educational program of the school since the factor of cultural homogeneity, which appears to be so basic to successful learning, can in this fashion be encouraged. At the same time, regional differences are so great that I assume the degree of transfer-ability of one such program more or less intact from one place to another may not be very high.

Linguistics and Teaching Materials in Reading

I should like now to move to the question of the contributions of linguistics to the development of teaching materials in reading. Linguistics is a term standing for any one of a large number of ways of inquiring into the processes of human language. It is a venerable academic discipline, although its impact upon schooling is very recent. Today many school people think that linguists hold *the* answer to all our problems. That there are important concepts which may help us immeasurably in planning for the development of teaching materials is true enough; however, the linguist is not an educator, and we should be cautious in evaluating any suggestions he makes regarding the direct classroom application of those ideas. Rarely is the linguist himself qualified to weigh the social, cultural, and psychological factors that modulate effective teaching and learning.

In retrospect, we may note that the initial contribution of linguistic analysis in the preparation of teaching materials began a dozen or so years ago with suggestions as to how certain linguistic principles might be applied in the construction of reading and language textbooks. These applications were utilized by both sides of the usual "teaching-to-read-argument"; namely, to the preparation of materials based on the principle of learning by synthesis, phonics approaches, or learning by analysis—the "whole-word" approach. While linguists have had more to say to the devotee of phonics approaches, the point that requires emphasis is that these early contributions were primarily applications to the kinds of materials already available and in use. These represent, as well, the dominant teaching materials and approaches to learning to read used in schools today, as has already been noted. In addition, they probably represent the high-water mark of direct participation by linguists themselves in the preparation of teaching materials per se.

The more important contributions of linguistics are now at hand and waiting to be applied in practice, and much more will be available to us as the years go by. These contributions, however, deal more with the nature of child language, its development, and its differences and similarities within various ethnic and racial groups as those differences are expressed, particularly in the oral language. From these findings powerful ideas for guiding us to new approaches in raising levels of literacy may, I believe, be derived.

Here are some major generalizations which I derive from linguistic research, followed by some implications for practice that go far beyond finding ways to individualize instruction, given existing teaching materials:

1. The oral language sits at the base of all subsequent language learning. This suggests major emphasis should be placed upon helping children expand that language. It also follows that, since language is one mode of expression for representing, recalling, or otherwise reflecting experience,

the kinds and quality of the school experience become a central concern in enhancing literacy.

2. All human beings possess a natural proclivity for language. No child growing up in a culture where there is at least one other person with whom to speak will fail to acquire the abilities to speak and listen. In all reasonably normal development, the speed and complexity with which that process of acquisition occurs is nothing short of a miracle.

3. Systems for recording oral language (through printed words or some other means of graphic representation, as in handwriting) are closely related to the oral language. In many respects they can be viewed as natural extensions of the oral language; and it may be reasonably assumed that there are inner structures which allow reading and writing to emerge much as the ability to speak and listen develop.

4. Language derives from individual experiences; its development, which depends upon those experiences, is uniquely individualistic in its emergence. While we can map development of language—and hence, of reading—such mapping can consequently be done only in very broad sweeps. Common vocabularies, lists of skills, and other abilities that purport to represent development at best represent only averages plus guesses of 'what comes first and what may follow.

5. Language processing is an extraordinarily complex behavior about which we actually know very little. We do know that it would be impossible to find the time to teach even a fraction of the various skills, abilities, and other capacities that are evoked when the desire to read or speak is present. Our problem in devising teaching materials is to determine what is important in learning to read. Since reading is a behavior that cannot be observed directly—we must devise schemes or strategies for determining if reading has occurred—we may safely assume that the interior wants, needs, and feelings of the individual deserve priority consideration.

6. Language abilities are interrelated. Growth in one ability apparently has powerful effects upon the other language functions. That growth is primarily dependent upon the stimulation of thought processes. Therefore, the meaningful units in language processing are not words more or less in isolation, they are comprised of strings of words: phrases, sentences, and other longer, more meaningful units.

7. Language is a personal matter reflecting the innermost feelings of self-worth and individual competence. Criticism of that language, expressed or implied, strikes deeply, quickly, and in many instances with devastating negative effect.

Teaching Materials in Schools
with Large Minority Populations

Teaching materials that will help resolve the very serious problems of reading and other language deficiencies in schools populated predominantly by children from racial and ethnic minorities consequently are not basically different from those I would recommend for any school situation. One qualifier is important. In schools with minority populations, it is mandatory that these materials be in the hands of a teaching staff whose attitudes, language, and values are roughly similar to those of the student body. The situation would then parallel the one in those majority schools in the country that are said to reflect the American middle-class culture and its value system. At the same time, I would emphasize that while there is great need for restructuring language programs in general, and reading instruction in particular, it is in these minority situations where the problem is especially crucial. Drawing upon the previously noted linguistically derived ideas, the following principles reflect my thinking with regard to the appropriate kinds of teaching materials for such situations:

1. The language of the child must not only be respected, it must become the vehicle for communication and thought in the school setting. It is the prime teaching material.

2. Since the development of reading (and other language) abilities is in many respects idiosyncratic, teaching materials must be sufficiently flexible to be utilized in an individualized program of instruction. As previously noted, grouping according to achievement is neither necessary nor desirable except as a convenience to the teacher. Moreover, the effects of achievement grouping both on actual progress in learning and on attitudes toward learning demonstrate that there is no advantage, and probably considerable disadvantage to the learner, when he is so grouped, either between or within classes. Teacher convenience can no longer be defended as a reason for such a policy.

3. Probably the most effective concrete teaching material in the early stages of learning to read is derived from the experiences and language of the child, individually recorded first by the teacher and subsequently written by the youngster himself.

4. The child who develops competencies in writing his own language will move to materials prepared by others easily and satisfactorily *if* attention is given primarily to thinking processes, to ideas, and to feelings rather than to specific meanings of words, spelling, correctness of gramma-

tical form, and the like. Indeed, the place of such correctness is open to serious question until such time as the child is capable of reading and writing with considerable fluency; even then it probably should be used most sparingly, if at all.

5. The everyday world of newspapers, magazines, and pamphlets, along with the self-production of children and the world of children's literature, form the most remarkable and functional resources of teaching materials available. Most present-day materials designed solely for the teaching of reading provide pale resources when placed alongside these relevant and meaningful materials.

6. Principles and materials effective in early language instruction are effective at remedial levels and should find application at all stages of instruction.

The Question of Teaching Materials: A Retrospective View

My view of the situation, then, is that we must first learn how to individualize instruction within a framework in which the child, his language, and his experience are seen to be worthy avenues for enhancing learning. Within that approach, we draw upon the primary teaching resource in the enhancement of language in all its forms: the experience of the individual child. That experience is not simply what has happened to the child out of school, important as that may be. It includes all of the happenings arranged for him by his teacher and his school. Thus the teaching materials are the people he knows, the places he can be taken to, the literature he hears, and all the other sources of information and ideas we can make available to him. From such experiences a sympathetic and understanding teacher helps the child express ideas and thoughts and feelings. His oral language, providing the base for all future language development, in the initial (as well as in the remedial) stage becomes the first source of words to be written and read. Subsequently, when the child reads things written by others, the most useful materials will be those that are congruent with the interests and experience background of the child. Gradually, we would expect to see each child expand his awareness of the world through reading books of many different kinds. However, this means we must find ways to secure these books so that children can read them. Thirty-five books with one title, as we now have in the standard textbook, regardless of the quality of the literary selections contained therein, surely is a meager source compared to that available in thirty-five different books selected from the vast field of children's literature. For the sake of bringing higher quality and greater variety to the classroom, I believe that the "true textbook" is not a textbook in the conventional sense at all, but a book written by an artist experienced in his subject matter who is sensitive to the needs and interests of children.

The Problem for Teacher Education

Education is one of the more conservative institutions; its resistance to change is widely recognized and is the subject of much frustration among those who would seek to reform it.[9] But change and innovation in the area of reading are even more resistant to reform, a situation brought about because of the close interconnections that have been built over the past thirty or more years between publishers and those who have either written or consulted in the preparation of the teaching materials themselves. It is common knowledge that many of the most prestigious names in the field of reading have lent their time and talents to the publishing industry, not without considerable reward to themselves. In their turn, publishing houses have invested tens of millions of dollars in their products.[10] It is true that many of those whose names grace the title pages of such materials have modified their views with respect to what constitutes an appropriate instructional program. A few have always held divergent views from those expressed in the pages of the textbooks but have associated themselves with these materials because they have honestly believed that the sheer problem of numbers of children and teachers required that pragmatic solutions be applied in any attempt to deal effectively with the problem of teaching reading. Still, over the years the effect has been that strong alliances and interconnections have been forged between large numbers of collegiate-level reading specialists, the public schools, and the publishers. Myths and rituals about the best ways to teach reading have in this course of events evolved that serve to protect the status quo. Consequently it is now generally but erroneously thought, in this country at

[9] Silberman, op. cit.

[10] In all fairness, it must be pointed out that the publishers by and large honestly believe their products to be good and useful. They have heeded the advice of expert opinion and have attempted to provide the profession with what it wanted. The problem, of course, is that such programs become institutionalized to such an extent they lag seriously behind new knowledge and the applications of that knowledge in practical situations.

least, that reading cannot be taught without placing major reliance upon one or more of these published materials.

In the face of this situation, which at times seems so overwhelming that little or nothing can be done, I have attempted to present information which can be used to restructure programs designed to prepare teachers who would evoke effective reading behavior, particularly with regard to those children who are members of social groups where reading and language problems are endemic. I reiterate: No child need be denied the ability to read and write with the proficiency his experience and capacity for thought allows. The problem of getting him to that point is indeed almost insurmountable unless we take such action as is necessary to break up the monopoly which traditional approaches to the teaching of reading now exercise in this country. I believe this monopoly presents a problem to education at large, of course, but I am dismayed at the extraordinary effect it has upon children living in our slums and ghettos.

The problem for teacher education, then, is to get to these new ideas. That they can produce the kinds of results we desire is already amply illustrated. For example, I refer to such sensitive pieces as those appearing in Herbert Kohl's and Victor Hernandez Cruz' book of selections written by young children, entitled *Stuff*.[11] Another is "The Children of Cardozo Tell It Like It Is," a collection of pictures and stories written by children following the riots in Washington, D.C.[12] Or sample James Herndon's *The Way It Spozed to Be*[13] or the many brilliant, varied, and sensitive works coming from the Watts Writer's Workshops over the past several years under the guidance and direction of Budd Schulberg. And of course there is the very popular book by Sylvia Ashton-Warner called *Teacher*.[14]

But just how does one get there, if indeed one sees it as a desirable goal? It requires us to change our attitudes toward language and how it functions in relation to thought. In the face of many presumptions about the importance of absolutes in language—minimum standards of grammatical usage, proper pronunciation, precise knowledge of words, knowledge of rules—we need to shift our attention to the interior being. In shifting our focus, we discover that there is value in the child's ideas and in the language he uses to express those ideas—limited, unstandard, or inappro-

[11] Herbert Kohl and Victor Hernandez Cruz, eds., *Stuff* (New York: World Publishing Co., 1970).

[12] *The Children of Cardozo Tell It Like It Is*, (Newton, Mass.: Educational Development Laboratories, 1970).

[13] James Herndon, *The Way It Spozed To Be* (New York: Simon & Schuster, 1968).

[14] Sylvia Ashton-Warner, *Teacher* (New York: Simon & Schuster, 1963).

priate as it may appear to be in polite company—or at least where so-called standard English is commonly employed. And, in finding such value, we also are letting the child in on the secret! These ideas and that language are the raw materials in all language learning. It is self-evident, if not a happy realization to have to come by, that setting minimum standards for language in the classroom, sets the minority child on the path followed by so many of his predecessors. That path leads the child away from that place—the school—which he has found is "not for real," because he cannot function successfully there. Primarily, he cannot function successfully because his language, and therefore himself as a person, is not acceptable.

The problem for teacher education is therefore very great. Teacher educators can no longer allow cookbook courses that prepare teachers to use existing materials. While it is important to know what is available along textbook lines, if only to decide what not to use in the classroom, it is much more necessary to understand the basic ingredients in the teaching of reading: knowledge about language development and language learning, how the child's own language can be used to enhance that development, and such sources of richly rewarding reading as are available in trade books (or children's literature). Concomitantly, ways of teaching with these tools must be individualized.

I have proposed many ideas and suggested practices that are, it would seem, diametrically opposed to what we are attuned to in teacher education. I would add, however, that very little of what I have had to say is all that new. You will find many of these ideas in a book written in 1936 by Nila Banton Smith entitled *American Reading Instruction*.[15] These themes have emerged repeatedly for more than forty years. Such evidence persists to remind us that tradition dies hard and that the field of reading particularly is encrusted with it. Perhaps we are entering a time when the kind of dynamic leadership will emerge that can provide the curriculum revision needed at the college level and the courage necessary to get knowledge into practice.

[15] Nila Banton Smith, *American Reading Instruction* (Morristown, N.J.: Silver Burdett & Co., 1936).

10

BLACK REFLECTIONS ON THE CULTURAL RAMIFICATIONS OF IDENTITY

VINCENT HARDING

"When I know who I am . . ."

First Thoughts

It is dangerous to speak seriously of the power of "identity" in the presence of an oppressed and colonized people—even if the ultimate issues are camouflaged by vague and seemingly harmless references to "cultural" ramifications. For the movement among nonwhite peoples toward authentic identity is the starting point of all struggle against those imposed structures of a dominating society which warp the vision of our selfhood, crush us inexorably downward, and threaten ultimately to destroy our spirits—to say nothing of our flesh. No educator must come to this issue without recognizing that among the wretched of the earth the beginning of knowledge and affirmation of self is also the beginning of a long battle against the systems which created the domination, and that the educational system is crucial.

This was a central message of our black classic, *Invisible Man*,[1] pressed

[1] Ralph Ellison, *Invisible Man* (New York: Random House, 1947).

[103

forward most precisely in that chapter which describes the hospital of the white world. The nameless Black Everyman who was the protagonist of the novel had been taken to the hospital to recover from (and be cured of) the mishap which had occurred during his first struggle-encounter with the heart of America's industrial world. In the course of the encounter in the white factory it had become clear to the keepers of the factory that Everyman could not become of fullest use to them unless he were broken from his own black past, made incapable of the anger which flows naturally out of that past (and present), and thereby made a neuter entity. That was why he was sent to the hospital. (In other, more relevant words, the hospital was to carry out the role of the American educational system.)

With that mission in mind, the white hospital staff placed Black Everyman in a lucite box which was frighteningly reminiscent of a coffin, put on his head "a piece of cold metal like the cap worn by an occupant of an electric chair" and attached similar electric nodes to his stomach. Then to the accompaniment of the strains of Beethoven's *Fifth*, the electrode system burned into his brain and into his guts until they racked him to the point where he could remember neither his own name nor the name of his mother, the point beyond anger where only bewilderment reigned, his eyes filled with tears and his mouth with blood. The institution which was supposed to heal was tearing him apart from himself so that he might ultimately better serve the purposes of the keepers of the factory (who seemed strangely identical with the directors of the hospital). Nevertheless, it was in the midst of this experience that Black Everyman formed within his tortured mind the words which must break into the presence of any serious discussion of identity. He said to himself, "When I know who I am, then I'll be free."

It is not surprising that we should be set so firmly upon the pathway to an understanding of the issues of identify and freedom through the medium of Ralph Ellison's masterpiece, for his work represents in a quintessential way that sensitivity to the crucial issues of Black life and death—of Black indentity—which is characteristic of our best artists. It was in the fullness of that realization that another Black creator wrote:

> If you should see a Man
> walking down a crowded
> street
>   talking
>   Aloud

To Himself
Don't run
in The
Opposite Direction
But run
Toward Him
for he is a
Poet
You have Nothing to
Fear
From the
Poet
But The
Truth[2]

These reflections on identity and the power of its meaning are informed by such men (and women) and their search for truth. Ellison is the beginning point.

Ellison on Identity: Roots and Ramification

Through the pages of *Invisible Man* we are introduced to "ramifications" of Black identity which carry all the power that such a word in our mind. But we are also reminded that for an oppressed people there is no separation of "culture" from politics, from economics, from lifelong struggle toward freedom.

Appropriately enough then, the search to affirm identity and integrity begins with the grandfather of Black Everyman, a person whose identity has evidently been that of a clownish, grinning Uncle Tom in the eyes of the white (and Black) world. But on the grandfather's deathbed it is revealed to the family what the true self-vision has been, for the dying man tells the boy, "... our life is a war and I have been a ... spy in the enemy's country .... I want you to overcome 'em with yeses, undermine 'em with grins, agree 'em to death and destruction, let 'em swoller you till they vomit or bust wide open." Thus the politics of racial oppression creates identities which cannot be freed except through the power of death.

[2] Ted Joans, "The Truth," *Black Pow-Wow* (New York: Hill & Wang, 1969), p.1. Reprinted by permission of Hill & Wang, A Division of Farrar, Straus and Giroux, Inc. Copyright ©1969 by Ted Joans.

With this memory in mind, the young Everyman goes forth to seek his own self-vision. Early on he is forced by the white world to enter into that false identity in which Black boys (and it is only as we remain boys in spirit that this can work) fight and maul each other in a battle royal for the electrified pennies of the white world. This is obviously the identity of each Black man for himself, of fights over poverty programs, institutional promotions, and foundation grants, of internecine warfare, of eternal adolescence. And its consequences are obvious. Its ramifications are the ramifications of stunted spirits and the emergence of jagged distrust within the communities of the oppressed. Therefore its results are continued oppression often under the guise of charity.

It is with the blood of this struggle against the brothers still in his mouth that Everyman seeks another pathway to identity, one long familiar to the colonized peoples of the world. He is academically successful in the white society's school for colored children, and makes the graduation speech at the end of that journey. It is a speech obviously meant to please the white benefactor-rulers, filled with Booker T. Washingtonisms, redolent with attitudes and viewpoints which he assumes they want to hear from him. He discovers that they would really prefer to see him fight other Black people; but when the speech is finally allowed, Everyman discovers that if he is not to become a participant in a continous Black battle royal, if he is to take seriously the education afforded by the white world, then he must prepare to function according to their image. His identity must be that of servant (often white collar and graduate degree) to that world.

Here again, the ramifications are essentially political, for while the oppressor speaks of his interest in the culture and the speeches of the native, while white America claimed (especially as cities were burning) a new devotion to Black culture, what is really being discussed are the mechanisms of control, the creation of better servants, the development of more battles royal. Neither equality nor pluralism is of any real consequence in their minds.

Not until Everyman begins to see the contradictions of the white world, begins to sense the possible authentic power (another word for identity) of the black world in Harlem does he begin to be potentially dangerous. It is at that point that his new insights eventually lead to a situation in which he upsets some of the machinery in the white paint factory, a factory whose motto is "Keep America Pure with Liberty Paints." He obviously must be readjusted. So that is when he is placed in the white hospital, innundated and overwhelmed by the electronic brain- (and gut-)washing processes (did Ellison foresee the powers of television?), and made fit for employment in the processes of keeping America pure.

Fortuately, there is a potential power of Black identity which cannot be overcome, even by electrodes and Beethoven. Thus it is in the Black community, living its life, eating its food, fighting its battles (but, strangely enough, not deeply loving and enjoying its women), that Everyman again moves toward authentic Black identity, and discovers that such identity preordains struggle and conflict with the systems of white America. For while living and eating, celebrating and loving in the heart of one's people is a pathway toward identity which may be called "cultural," if those people lie on the precipice of life and under the constant blows of exploitation and the threat of destruction, it becomes clear that larger struggle for life and breath—and for identity itself—is at the heart of the matter.

In other words, if a Black man says, "When I know who I am, then I'll be free," the question must follow, free for what? And the answers pour forth like a flood: free for the struggles toward authentic, self-determining life, free to vindicate the lives of the fathers whom we now affirm, free to build a new world beyond such oppression as our fathers suffered, free to build a new life for the children.

That is the burden and the privilege of true identity among the oppressed. It is never private (although it is personal) and cannot ultimately be found in deeply subjective trips into the castles of our skin. That is a Western understanding of identity. Rather, ours must be found in the context of the Black community—past, present, and future—in the community of the oppressed and their cause. That is why the school systems of the dominating society do not really encourage authentic Black identity. Instead they teach that the pathway to truly humane identity is through some white-painted "universalism," an amorphous cloud which effectively separates us from the struggles of our fathers and the cries of our children for life.

Partly because of such education, and partly for far more earthy reasons, Ellison's Everyman attempts to lift his newly found passion for the life of his people to a "higher" level by seeking his identity and allegiances with a "universal" white-controlled Brotherhood (one may translate freely: Western Christian Church or Western-controlled Communist Party). Not unexpectedly, both he and the struggle of his people are betrayed by the Brotherhood. Not only do they deny his culture, and therefore his identity (even while their women grasp feverishly at his Black sexualtiy), but they ultimately deny his politics and his responsibility as a Black man for the leadership of his people. They refuse, in other words, to recognize the generation-binding quality of true identity.

So, driven again into the midst of his people, Black Everyman is now suspect, although he really wishes to give himself to their struggle. He has wandered too long in the hospitals, meeting-rooms, and bedrooms of white America for those persons honestly seeking to lead the struggle of the black masses to trust him. (They have no such identity—problems—save, perhaps, whether they shall be Ras the Exhorter only, or finally allow themselves to be driven to become Ras the Destroyer. But always Ras, Black to the bone, Black to Ethiopia's bones.)

It is clear now where he will end. After a brief period of identityless exploitation of other black people, Everyman is lost. He is driven underground not as a result of his discovery of identity in the midst of the struggle for his people, but as a result of his failure to discover who he is. Perhaps the hospital finally conquered. For though he appears on his way back above ground in a strange, dream-like sequence at the end of the novel, he is obviously without purpose or direction, mouthing those empty universalisms which regularly break forth from the lives of those whose identity is lost, strayed, or stolen.

Perhaps the refrain from the blues which ran through the novel was really more deeply ingrained in Everyman than even he could admit. Perhaps his basic question still remained: "What did I do to be so black and blue?"

Understandably, Ellison could not carry us beyond his own limits in the search for authentic identity, and his limits were the parameters of the black community he knew best, the community here. Identity was to be sought only in this land, on these shores, in the midst of the mind-purging hospitals and whitening factories of America. That was why Everyman could not understand Ras the Exhorter. That, perhaps, was why there were no answers for Everyman beyond the answers imposed by this strange land.

Beyond Ellison, Beyond Hospitals: The Poets

We are no longer so limited in the cultural expressions of Black artists now that the search for identity—as expressed by the artists of our people—is one with deep roots into the experiences of our African forefathers while always affirming our fathers on these shores. Some suggestion of the power of the search (and the discovery) is available through Joans in "O Great Black Masque":

O great black masque that is me
that travels with me in spirit
your big eyes that see tomorrows
saw yesterdays and gazes at now
O great black masque of my soul
those ears have heard the clink
of slaves chains and the moans
of sorrow of our past but those
same ears can hear our now
O great black masque that is me
you who copulated with Europe's science
and now dynamically demysterfies Europe
O great black masque who is our
ancestors with your cave mouth
filled with sharp teeth to chew
the ropes that bind our hands and minds
O great black masque you that grins
you that always wins the thrower of
seven cowries and two black eyed dice
O great black masque who says that it
half past pink since white is not a color
O great black masque that carried me from Bouake
to Alabama and back From Mali to Manhattan
O great black masque that dances in me day and night
O black masque of urban guerillas and forest gorillas
O black masque that screams in joy at childbirth and
opens up to the rays of the sun O great black masque
your sharp blade tongue burns war makers buildings
You who stand guard to African breast and soul
O great black masque give us our blacker heavens/
release our minds from borrowed white hells/ O great
black masque of Africa O great black masque of all
black people O beautiful black masque Our own black
truth[3]

For the Black community today, Joans reminds us, there is no identity without the spirit and roots of the mother continent. This was what Everyman missed. And in this affirmation of beginnings, there is also an African sense of timelessness, a sense of the continuity of our life with

[3] Ted Joans, "O Great Black Masque," *Black Pow-Wow* (New York; Hill & Wang, 1969), p. 5. Reprinted by permission of Hill & Wang, A Division of Farrar, Straus and Giroux, Inc. Copyright ©1969 by Ted Joans.

that of the fathers and the unborn children. There is a solid sense of confidence, in the midst of all the Middle Passages of our beings, that our spirit will endure and prevail, linked as we are with the spirits of our homeland.

But one sees clearly in Joans that this is no mere "cultural" or "spiritual" identity. It is about struggle for integrity and multileveled freedom. It is about guerillas and gorillas, about the burning of the war-makers' buildings. It is a deep concern over the ultimate liberation of Africa itself. Above all it is about the struggle to "release our minds from borrowed white hells." In its most profoundly political sense, it is about release from essential identification with the goals and purposes of America.

White hospitals, white hells, white systems of domination—these are the enemies of our fathers and our children. The search for identity in the Black communtiy now leads inexorably to such conclusions. That is the meaning of Mari Evans:

> Speak the Truth to the people
> To identify the enemy is to free the mind
> Free the mind of the people
> Speak to the mind of the people
> Speak truth.[4]

When we know who we are, then we shall be free, Everyman told us—without being able to appropriate that freedom himself. But the word flows the other way as well. We shall know who we are and what we are for when we are free. This is the ultimate ramification of identity: the freedom to be and to do what we are for—the sense of vocation in the deepest, religious meaning of that word. To understand who we are, then, is to understand our "calling."

In the struggle toward identity, that "calling" comes not simply through the apprehension of some voice from the world of the invisible (though that surely may be included among non-Western peoples), but it is wrested out of a growing recognition of who our fathers and our children are, who we are, and what is the reality of the enemy systems which have been used against them and against us. By now it is clear that the latter reality is focused in all the hospitals and hells which have taken from

---

[4] Mari Evans, "Speak the Truth to the People," *I Am a Black Woman* (New York: William Morrow, 1970), pp. 91-92. Reprinted by permission of the author and publisher.

major segments of black people any full sense of identity and therefore any hope for freedom. It also should be clear that the creators of these institutions are not really planning to provide new institutions to encourage that "beauty full of healing" which our lives so badly need.

Therefore our calling now is to create new institutions, even while we struggle against the powers of the old. Our release will not come without such struggles and such building. Our identity and our calling will continue to be manufactured under white control until, as Langston Hughes said, "we learn how to bake"—and learn how to secure the products of our creation. That is why Mari Evans could say:

> A free mind has no need to scream
> A free mind is ready for other things
> To BUILD black schools
> To BUILD black children
> To BUILD black minds
> To BUILD black love
> To BUILD black impregnability
> To BUILD a strong black nation
> To BUILD.[5]

All of this building is cultural, all of it is political, all of it is necessarily economic, and the spiritual suffuses its entire being. All of it grows out of a sense of authentic identity (see, for instance, the title of Miss Evans' book: *I Am a Black Woman*) which frees the mind. For those who would take the risk of developing Black children with minds free to live and die for their community, the institutions we create (within and outside the white systems) must begin with that community. They must be institutions which immerse themselves in an understanding of that community, which legitimize its healthy manifestations and clarify the sources of its sickness. The roots of the community here and beyond the seas must be explored and understood.

All teaching ultimately must flow out of the resources and the needs of the ancestral community, returning what has been created by the fathers into the lives of the children, helping them to provide what is not yet present for the good of the whole. Skills of every kind must be developed, but skills must always follow spirit. Both are necessary, but the attitudes and frames of mind must come out of the best creations of the Black community, and only those who are ready to know and learn and affirm

[5] Ibid.

that community are ready to teach our children, are ready to build new institutions for our children. In such a setting, Joans becomes more than humorist when he writes:

BLACK PEOPLE
I see Black People
I hear Black People
I smell Black People
I taste Black People
I touch Black People
Black People is my Momma
Black People is my Dad
Black People is my Sister, Brother, Uncle, Aunt and Cousins
Black People is all we Black People ever had
Now that we the Black People know that
We the Black People should be glad[6]

No Black people can believe in pluralism without believing in Black People. When this becomes a reality of identity in our minds, then those who now work within the present systems and who seek to build anew for our people must perforce circumvent and subvert the white nationalist purposes and goals of the hospitals and hells. Breaking constantly against their commitments to the white American way of life, the new creator-builders must introduce into their classrooms all the Black texts which are now not approved. They must use the resources—human, artistic, and institutional—of the Black community as basic curriculum, considering all else as extraneous, occasionally necessary evils at best.

The task is a difficult one: While teaching children how to pass the tests of a dominating, antiblack system, one must create a new self-affirming substance within the spirits of the students which will lead step-by-step to the breaking of the power of domination. While some of us must build outside the immediate physical presence of the prevailing white systems, most others must struggle from within—but struggle with a sense of identity, purpose, and direction—always turned toward the needs of our people to overcome the systems of oppression. Education, from preschool on up, thereby becomes highly political, participates in the age-old struggles of our people for self-determination and self-definition. All teachers

[6] Ted Joans, "Black People," *Black Pow-Wow* (New York: Hill & Wang, 1969), p. 75. Reprinted by permission of Hill & Wang, A Division of Farrar, Straus and Giroux, Inc. Copyright © 1969 by Ted Joans.

become members of a new politico-religious force, dedicated to the release of every black mind from "borrowed white hells." Teachers who find their own identity thereby find their own dangerous—but glorious—calling.

Pluralism, as a next, but not ultimate, stage must be wrested from the white nationalist systems of today. A new order must come to birth within the smothering belly of the old, with all the dangerous tensions involved. Chances must be taken, experiments must be carried out, jobs must be risked, organizing must be done, Black battles royal must be banished. There can be no real integrity/identity achieved (on personal or communal levels) without these things. Release cannot come without hard, persistent, organized struggle. Hells and hospitals do not give up their domain without struggle. But unless that release comes, and unless new humane systems of life and growth are developed, the identity of no man will be secured and we shall be fated to wander with Black Everyman in the sewers (bomb and pollution shelters?) of the Western world.

This is the ultimate ramification of identity for the black community— and, I suspect, for all the communities of the white-ravaged peoples of the world. We discover who we are and thereby discover what we are for. We are for a new society. We are for the prevailing of a spirit represented more by Africa than by Europe-America. To know who we are is to begin to move toward our real work, our real calling. It is to hear Don Lee and to say with him:

> "blackpeople
> are moving, moving to return
>   this earth into the hands of
> human beings."[7]

---

[7] Don Lee, "A Message All Black People Can Dig (& a few negroes too)," *Don't Cry, Scream* (Detroit: Broadside Press, 1969), p. 64. Reprinted by permission of the author and the publisher.

11

ETHNIC AND BILINGUAL EDUCATION FOR CULTURAL PLURALISM

EDUARDO SEDA BONILLA

Four years have elapsed since the First Puerto Rican Conference, sponsored in 1967 by New York City's Mayor John Lindsay, adopted my proposal for "A Second Look at Cultural Pluralism."[1] Cultural pluralism was conceived as the antidote against racism in this society. The logic of my argument was developed along the following lines:[2]

There have been two possible ways of "adaptation" for minority groups in the United States. One way was designed for the ethnic white minorities, the immigrants of different nationalities. The other way of "adaptation" was reserved for the nonwhite ethnic minorities: the Blacks, the Indians, the Chicanos, and the Puerto Ricans. For the white minorities, the adaptation started at a low point of contact with America: a point in which the group boundaries—the differences—were drawn according to ethnic or cultural characteristics in contrast with the surrounding "American way of life." These differences were defined by country of origin (Italy, Ireland, and Germany), by languages, and by religion (Jewish, Catholic). Literature (novels, stories, poems) and movies nostalgically

[1] "A Second Look at Cultural Pluralism," in *Revista de Extramuros* (University of Puerto Rico), 1968, and in *Requiem por una Cultura* (San Juan: Edil Press, 1969).
[2] "Ethnic Studies and Cultural Pluralism," in *Memoirs of XXXIX International Congress of Americanists*, Lima, Peru, July, 1970.

describe the passing away of the immigrants' way of life, often beautiful and rich with the flavor of centuries-old emotional ties. The life experience these immigrants brought in their culture was condemned to disappear as they sailed past the Statue of Liberty into the melting pot where the "greenhorn customs" were washed away to create "full-blooded Americans."

Little Italies, Germantowns, Irish Shantytowns, and Frenchtowns flourished throughout America, and when their inhabitants, the "natives" of those slums, had become "American" enough, most of them moved away, leaving their golden streets for another type of minority group: the racially discriminated group who must remain to inherit the filthy, overcrowded, crumbling tenements left behind by the "ethnics" as they dove into the melting pot to search for the American Dream.

A question often asked rhetorically of Puerto Ricans, as if we were the first and not the second type of minority, is why have we not dipped ourselves, like other peoples, into the melting pot in search of the American Dream so as to begin climbing the social ladder to success. The same question, however, could be asked of other groups: Blacks, Mexicans, Amerindians. The answer to this question lies in the fact that these are groups differentiated from the North American majority on the basis of racial criteria.

There is an insidious hypocrisy in dealing with the problem of racial minorities as if they were just another ethnic group, e.g., Germans, Italians, Irish, or any other minority group differentiated by the majority on the basis of ethnic and not racial characteristics. The argument that with time these groups will follow the same pattern as the ethnic minorities crashed against the harsh reality that most ethnic minorities entered the American society at a later date than Blacks and Mexicans. The Amerindians were here before the whites decided to call it America in honor of an obscure cartographer from Italy. The Spaniards inhabited this continent which they called The Indies from the early sixteenth century. Mexicans were brought into the United States with the conquest of their territory in the middle of the nineteenth century. The Blacks were certainly here longer than the Irish, the Germans, the Italians. The racial minorities have had more than ample time if they really were to be accepted as part of the melting-pot stew.

In the United States the acculturation of Blacks, Mexicans, Puerto Ricans, and those who are nonwhite signifies their adoption of an inferior noxious identity. Thus they acquire a stigmatized self-image, and in taking in a noxious identity lose their cultural autonomy and vitality.[3] Giving up their cultural integrity and moving along the path of acculturation does not lead to social assimilation. At the very gates of the establishment, their cultural credentials are denied recognition on the grounds of their "racial" inferiority.

Acculturation does not wash away the stigma after they give up their cultural identity and take on American ways. The only alternative left to some members of this group is for them to break into the silent majority by means of "passing," that is, crossing the racial boundaries at an unguarded point and remaining there as social incognito. The difference for racial minorities, in other words, remains after acculturation and the only way to full assimilation is then to "pass": to break completely with the ethnic community, the family, and the past while adopting a false identity.

When the ethnic (cultural) identity of racially differentiated minorities gives way before the acculturative pressure imposed by the North American society, they fall into an empty social space, into a marginality that Mexicans fill with the aberration of the Pocho, Blacks with the "coolcat," Indians with religious revival movements such as the sun dance, and Puerto Ricans with the "men." Once the ethnic identity breaks down, the defenses against the internalization of the dysnomia—that is, the spiritually harmful identification imbedded in the racistic norms of the culture—also are swept away. These groups are not accepted by the white silent majority on racial grounds and remain, when acculturated, marginal to the ethnic group and marginal to the silent (socially invisible) majority.

For the white minority, all they had to do to assimilate was to change the ethnic identification: discard their culture and become a silent and invisible part of the majority. A token recognition of their contribution remained as with spaghetti and knishes, which was then generalized in the melting pot for everybody else. Once their cultural identity subsided under the American cultural identity, the door to the silent or socially invisible world of the majority was open—because they were white. For those considered nonwhite, full participation in this society required a revision of the melting-pot theory and its substitution by cultural pluralism.

---

[3] "Therapeutic as well as reformist efforts verify the sad truth that in any system based on suppression, exclusion and exploitation, the suppressed, excluded and exploited unconsciously accept the evil image they are made to represent by those who are dominant." Erik H. Erickson, *Identity, Youth in Crisis* (New York: Norton, 1968), p. 59.

For the second type of minority group identified on the basis of a nonwhite racial stigma, shedding the ethnic identity that distinguished them from the American culture and taking over the American cultural identity, if anything, made things worse. It is well known that majority Americans offer greater respect and regard to a Black with a foreign accent styled after an alien way of life than to the native son. Perhaps deep in their hearts, majority Americans want the racially stigmatized groups to remain alien, to feel alien: out of sight, out of mind—with a memory of a home somewhere else where white Americans hope they will eventually return.

For this second type of minority, adaptation must be the reverse of the first type. The alternative to the melting-pot theory must be founded on cultural pluralism as a safeguard for nonwhite groups against the internalization of the stigma contained in the American culture. Racial minorities must overcome their self-depreciation by independent cultural assertion so they can contribute to the pluralistic society with their differences, thus creating beauty and diversity and not a similarity which transforms them into underdeveloped Americans, Piti-Yankees, Pochos, Uncle Toms, and whatnots. The ethnic attributes which distinguish these racial minorities from the silent (socially invisible) majority should serve as a bastion to sustain their integrity and self-respect, for the enrichment of their spiritual legacy. Their acculturation spells destruction and ruin for their creative potentialities and their contribution to this society. At this moment, the socially invisible and silent majority must help us in the effort to rediscover and strengthen our own cultural identity, or be faced with socially uprooted, disintegrated human beings unable to contribute their share to this society. Cultural pluralism for racial minorities must be accepted against the melting-pot theory which has been used with the white ethnic minorities if American society is to survive the crisis it is facing today.

During the last few years, we have witnessed the fascinating process of a reverse acculturation undertaken by Black Americans to an African cultural identity. An upsurge of energy and creativity has been released by the Blacks after their liberation from a culture in which their beauty and their creativity was denied. American Indians, Chicanos, and Puerto Ricans, although not yet totally acculturated in the Anglo culture, are rapidly learning the lesson taught by our Black brothers: to start not only to hold, but also to enrich and strengthen our own cultural identity and tradition.

Yet, an educational system based on the ethnocentric proposition that all men must be placed in the narrow mold of Americanization in order to become equals still is a roadblock, an obstruction to the access to higher education for students of racial minorities.[4] The educational system in its lower grades has functioned as an oppressive racist system to exclude Blacks, Puerto Ricans, Mexican Americans, and American Indians. At the upper levels of education cultural pluralism has been unself-consciously obtained, but it appears that in the lower levels of higher education there are still many limitations and shortcomings to the attainment of the multicultural model of man. We have very frequently heard among the students who now are entering college the bitter complaint against ethnocentrism and racist teachers who in some way attempted to instill in their minds a sense of inferiority which would produce failure in school and in life.

An educational system geared toward the goal of Americanization has become a gate to hell for Puerto Rican, Mexican, Black, and Amerindian students since it disintegrates their ethnic identity and forces in them the American way which spells self-hatred and dehumanized uprootedness. The most dramatic index of this stigmatization and colonization of the Puerto Rican student in New York is reflected in the following data.

According to a "Summary of Perceived Needs of the Puerto Rican Community" presented to a United States Senate Committee on Equal Educational Opportunities in 1960, of all Puerto Ricans twenty-five years of age or older, 87 percent have dropped out without graduating from high school. The rate of drop out for eighth grade was 52.9 percent. In 1968-1969, the dropout rate for Puerto Rican students by the twelfth year of schooling was 80 percent compared with 46 percent for Black students and 28.9 percent for Anglos. No more than 5 percent of Puerto Rican college-age youth are moving on to higher education, the rate for the Blacks being 15-20 percent and, for the general population, 45 percent. According to a report from Aspira (an organization for Puerto Ricans which works with the educational problems of Puerto Rican youths), the dropout rate for Puerto Ricans admitted to college is 60 percent.

In a report presented to the New York State Board of Regents in March, 1971, Mrs. Evelina Antonetty of the United Bronx Parent Association revealed that in the New York City public school system, there are

[4] This policy was carried to absurdity when English was imposed as the language of education in Puerto Rico at the outset of the American occupation in 1898. This policy was discontinued in 1948 by administrative subterfuge, not by a change in the law.

1.1 million students. Of these, 250,000 (25 percent) are Puerto Rican. Although 25 percent of the public school students in the city schools are Puerto Rican, only 3 percent (1,600) of the students who received academic diplomas from the city high schools in June, 1969, were Puerto Rican. Mrs. Antonetty comments that although 63 percent (nearly 20,000) of the students in School District 7 are Puerto Rican, there are only 3 principals and assistant principals out of a total of 91 who are Puerto Rican. In this same district, out of 1,580 teachers, only 55 are Puerto Rican or Cuban; of 32 guidance counselors, only 1 is Puerto Rican. Mrs. Antonetty rightfully asserts, "If one or two children are failing in a class perhaps there is something wrong with those children. But when 73 percent of a district are failing, there has to be something wrong with the schools."

The situation for Chicano students is quite similar to that of Puerto Ricans:

Statistics from the National Committee on Mexican American Education of the U.S. Office of Education dramatizes well the end result of educational policy that de-educates (Steiner):

In the Southwest the average Chicano child has only a 7th grade education.

The dropout, or push-out, rate in Texas for Chicano high school students is 89%, while in California 50% of Chicano high school students leave school between the 10th and 11th grade.

Along the Rio Grande Valley of Texas four out of five Chicano children fall two years behind their Anglo classmates by the 5th grade. (The city manager of San Antonio estimates that 44.3% of the barrio residents are "functionally illiterate;" 20% never went to school at all.)

College enrollment is infinitesimal. In California, where 14% of public school students are Chicanos, less than ½% of college students at the seven campuses of the University of California are Chicanos.[5]

Unless one takes a racistic position as a valid explanation for this tragic situation, one must seek its causes in the experiences of oppression and stigmatization that predispose students to failure and self-hatred by means of the self-fulfilling prophecy constantly imposed in their minds by racist teachers.

Ethnocentrism appears to have been highly prevalent among lower-middle-class people during the Nazi period, and teachers seem to have been

[5] Samuel Betances, *Proposal for HGSE to Establish a One Year Graduate Training Program for Puerto Rican and Chicano Educational Leaders*, Mimeographed, January 5, 1971.

one of the most militant groups in the Nazi movement.[6] To what extent ethnocentrism among teachers in the United States is the result of their lower-middle-class position or the result of faulty education is a question we do not need to answer. We cannot change anything about the socio-economic evaluation of people. We can change many of the educational processes they undergo in their professional formation.

So the question is: What can the higher education establishment do in the training of teachers to ameliorate ethnocentrism? The answer in my opinion lies in making ethnic studies programs a formal requirement in the training of teachers as well as other professionals who function as brokers mediating the relationship of ethnics with the dominant society. That also includes social workers, nurses, policemen, and candidates for the legal and medical professions.

Ethnic education and bilingualism are instrumentalities to reverse the causes of the injustices perpetrated by the dominant society on ethnic students. This approach attempts to strengthen their self-respect by making them aware of their history, their culture, their literature, and their outstanding figures, and by teaching them in the language which does not alienate them from their ethnic community. It also attempts to fill the information gap for other students in the university system. Bilingual programs attempt a reversal of the causes of injustice by teaching the student in the language in which he can best learn, as a precondition for equal opportunity in education.

The greatest danger is that these programs deny or ignore the fundamental purpose for which they were created; that is, the purpose of freeing the ethnic student from the cumulative degradation and stigmatization imposed on him by a racist society by making him aware of the causes of oppression, exploitation, and racism, and strengthening his ethnic identity. Upon accepting this liberalizing function, the university has begun its journey of return to the primordial sources which gave it its reason to be: That is to say, to return to its original source as an institution created for the noble purpose of liberating the human spirit through the knowledge of truth.

If these revindicating purposes are ignored or denied, the programs will fall into the hands of unscrupulous persons who will receive appointments by the adulation of students, and who will administer these programs like welfare programs, doling out grades and diplomas "free" without any other stipulation than that of not starting trouble. If the genuine purpose

[6] Hans Gerth, "The Nazi Party, Its Leadership and Composition," *American Journal of Sociology*, Vol. 45 (1940), pp. 517-541.

of the educational system upon creating these programs were not that of revindication, decolonization, and liberation, but that of falling in line with prebendaric corruptors, then the function of these programs would be without doubt an education in opportunism and bribery for the purpose of shutting up students so that they do not cause problems or create disorders. Thus, there would be lost forever an opportunity to create free consciences, inquisitive minds, men and women with a feeling of respect for universal values free from the double bind of an alienating identity. Without the integrity of an ethnic identity, the perspectives are obscure. This is equally true for Puerto Ricans, Chicanos, Indians, and Blacks. The opportunity to liberate the university from the Babylonic captivity into which it has fallen will have been lost. If the purpose of the university upon creating these programs is not liberation and affirmation of ethnic identity, the same will soon be converted into university slums, which will have to be eliminated when the ambient pestilence issuing from them becomes intolerable.

Among the questions of high priority in the establishment of ethnic studies programs and bilingual education is the need for a fund of knowledge attainable only by the means of empirical research. Thousands of dollars are now being spent in bilingual research mostly conducted, directed, and performed by people with little understanding of culture and language, and very little concern for the goal of cultural pluralism. As a matter of fact, bilingualism is used as a patronizing gesture, a special concession to a mentally retarded group—retarded, that is, in the "way" toward Americanization. I believe that such research in bilingual education, as well as the evaluation of educational methods and testing instrumentalities such as I.Q. and Proficiency Tests, must be conducted with a clear understanding of the fact that differences in culture imply differences in cognitive mapping, and that the test cannot be on mathematics to be graded on linguistics.

I believe that research in cognitive mappings of Puerto Ricans in different subcultures would constitute a great contribution to social science as well as, a great asset to the fund of knowledge necessary to strengthen bilingual and ethnic study programs. There is the possibility that a study on cognitive structure will be conducted among Mexican Americans. I see no reason why research of this kind could not be extended to Puerto Ricans and Blacks in New York, and to Amerindians throughout the nation.

12

ASIAN AMERICANS AND EDUCATION FOR CULTURAL PLURALISM

DON HATA, JR.

Who are the Asian Americans? If we rely on the textbooks and curriculum materials currently available, the answer is elusive at best. The fact is that very little is taught about the Asian Americans in our educational institutions—at all levels of instruction.

In contemporary America we find a wide range of peoples whose ancestry can be traced to almost every significant ethnic and national grouping in those lands which British imperialists once referred to as "east of Suez." Their total number is small—not quite one million—in proportion to the total population of the United States. They include Chinese, Japanese, and Koreans from east Asia; Indian, Pakistani, and other groups from south Asia; Vietnamese, Indonesians, Thais, Malaysians, Filipinos, and others from southeast Asia; and a wide representation of Pacific peoples such as Samoans, Guamanians, and native Hawaiians. Some are relatively new to the United States. Others, such as the Chinese and Japanese, can trace their roots in this nation to the early nineteenth

Acknowledgment is due the following persons for their assistance in the preparation of this paper: James Louie, Chairman of the Berkeley Asian American Education Task Force; and Edison Uno, lecturer, Asian American Studies Program at San Francisco State College.

[123

century.[1] But whether they are old or new additions to the American scene, all Asian Americans as well as Asians in Asia have remained largely ignored by educators and textbook authors.

Recently a number of standard United States history and social studies textbooks have been evaluated for their coverage of Asia and the Asian-American experience.[2] Texts were selected at random from levels of instruction ranging from elementary through college. The conclusions reached to date are grim: only a few have been judged to be adequate in their overall historical treatment. The Asian Americans were often completely omitted. In nearly every case they were not given fair treatment by the authors.[3]

A serious problem encountered in materials at all levels was that of inaccurate vocabulary. Many texts and their accompanying teacher's guides made no distinction between Asians in Asia and Asian Americans. Moreover, the term "Oriental" is still used instead of "Asian," which is more accurate and is preferred by Asian Americans. It would seem that educators who approve the use of these texts still view the world through the same perspective as those nineteenth century European imperialists who dismissed all areas east of Suez as the Orient, inhabited by uncivilized or otherwise inferior masses, and important only for economic exploitation and colonial adventurism. Obsolescent terms reflect the insensitivity and ignorance of their users, and both Asians and Asian Americans are

---

[1] According to the federal census of 1960 the three largest Asian American groups are the Japanese Americans (464,332), Chinese Americans (237,292), and Filipino Americans (176,310). The forthcoming publication of the 1970 census should indicate significant increases in the population of other groups, such as the Koreans, during the past decade.

[2] Evaluations are being conducted by special education committees of the Japanese American Citizens League as well as researchers at San Francisco State College and California State College, Dominguez Hills. See also Michael B. Kane's *Minorities In Textbooks* (Chicago: Quadrangle Books, 1970), pp. 122-130.

[3] Kane's survey, which was published in cooperation with the Anti-Defamation League of B'nai B'rith, found that "the present 1969 study is unable to report any significant changes in textbook presentations of this topic. Not one world history makes any overt reference to the presence of people of Oriental [*sic*] origin in the United States. Of the thirty American history and American problems and civics texts analyzed, two histories and eight problems and civics texts violate the criterion of *inclusion* by totally failing to mention this minority group. Furthermore, of the eleven American history and five social problems texts that mention Japanese Americans, none meets the dual criteria of *comprehensiveness* and *balance*. As a matter of fact, only two textbooks make references to either Chinese or Japanese Americans in contemporary society, and these are hardly to be considered complete." Ibid., p. 122.

reminded that even today many American educators perceive reality through the eyes of Rudyard Kipling.

There is a clear and present danger in the lumping together of Asians in Asia and Asian Americans, for it was this kind of confusion and false generalization which helped to create the hysterical appeal of anti-Chinese sentiment in late nineteenth century America. That appeal to racism manifested itself again in the evacuation and incarceration of Japanese Americans during World War II.[4] American attitudes toward Asian Americans have also closely reflected American relations with nations in Asia.[5]

Since the end of World War II, some authors have attempted to erase the volumes of pre-1945 hate literature which dealt with Asian Americans primarily in terms of how, where, and why they allegedly constituted a menace to American society.[6] In contrast to the alien and potentially

[4] During the spring and summer of 1942, 110,000 Japanese Americans on the West Coast " . . . alien and citizen, old and young, rich and poor—were evacuated to ten 'relocation centers,' barrack type communities surrounded by barbed wire and armed guards, located in inaccessible and largely barren areas in the interior of the United States from California to Arkansas." Roger Daniels and Harry H. L. Kitano, *American Racism: Exploration of the Nature of Prejudice* (Englewood Cliffs, N.J.: Prentice-Hall, 1970), p. 62. See also Audrie Girdner and Anne Loftis, *The Great Betrayal, The Evacuation of the Japanese Americans During World War II* (London: Macmillan, 1970); and Morton Grodzins, *Americans Betrayed, Politics and the Japanese Evacuation* (Chicago: University of Chicago Press, 1949).

[5] In *The Unwelcome Immigrant, The American Image of the Chinese, 1785-1882* (Berkeley: University of California Press, 1969), Stuart Creighton Miller reconstructs the negative image of the Chinese—as projected by early nineteenth century traders, diplomats, and missionaries—that preceded their actual arrival in the United States. The failure to distinguish between Chinese and Japanese Americans and their counterparts in Asia during the Yellow Peril hysteria after the turn of the century is summarized in William L. Neumann's *America Encounters Japan, From Perry to MacArthur* (New York: Harper and Row, 1963), pp. 212-227. A recent detailed study of the changing image of the Japanese Americans is Dennis Ogawa's *From Japs to Japanese: The Evolution of Japanese American Stereotypes* (Berkeley: McCutchan Press, 1971).

[6] In 1909 a series of publications appeared which added fuel to the alleged "Yellow Peril" and the growth of anti-Asian sentiment. The books of Homer Lea (the most sensational was *The Valor of Ignorance* which sold 18,000 copies before it went out of print in 1922) predicted that the Japanese would seize the entire Pacific Slope region. The San Francisco newspaperman Wallace Irwin created a widely believed stereotype of the typical Japanese immigrant in "Hashimura Togo." Irwin described Togo as a thirty-five-year-old "schoolboy" who spoke comical English, had prominent buckteeth, always smiled, and was ultra-polite; but underneath it all he was the "crafty Jap." See Neumann for a concise survey of other authors. Ibid., pp. 128-130.

subversive image which stereotyped the Japanese Americans before they proved their loyalty in bloody combat during World War II,[7] contemporary writers now hail them as Asian Horatio Algers who are "outwhiting the whites."[8] Many whites view the Japanese and other Asian Americans as members of a "model minority" whose docile and accommodationist posture should be emulated by more aggressive Blacks and Browns.[9] In response, many older members of the Asian American community have carefully avoided an active role in the postwar movement for increased civil rights. Seduced by the adulation heaped upon them by the white majority, and anxious to protect their new-found "acceptance," they are wary of activities which might identify them with other nonwhite minorities.[10]

But just as pre-World War II negative stereotypes were reflective of the isolationist attitude of the times, the recent positive images of the Asian American are also fleeting at best, especially in light of recent developments in foreign affairs. As the United States is forced to re-evaluate its relations with an increasingly powerful and economically competitive Japan and a China which no longer tolerates American meddling in its affairs, it is vital that a clear distinction be made between *Asians in Asia* and *Americans of Asian ancestry*. In reviewing the Japanese-American

[7] Segregated units of Japanese Americans such as the 100th Infantry Battalion and the 442nd Regimental Combat Team fought in the European Theater of Operations during World War II. Pentagon records indicate that the battle honors of these units made them the most decorated units in the entire history of the United States Army. Official Army statistics show that casualties comprised 314 percent of the units' original strength. See Chapter 23 entitled "Proof In Blood" in Bill Hosokawa's *NISEI: The Quiet Americans* (New York: Morrow and Co., 1969), pp. 393-422; and Orville C. Shirey, *Americans: The Story of the 442nd Combat Team* (Washington: Infantry Journal Press, 1946).

[8] "Success Story: Outwhiting the Whites," *Newsweek*, June 21, 1971, pp. 24-25.

[9] Harry H. L. Kitano warns against the easy application of the Japanese-American strategy of accommodation to the case of other minority groups in *Japanese Americans, The Evolution of A Subculture* (Englewood Cliffs, N.J.: Prentice-Hall, 1969), pp. xi-xii, 2-4.

[10] In the case of many Japanese Americans, memories of the abrupt mass evacuation, loss of property and possessions, and imprisonment without charges or a known date of release did little to inculcate faith in constitutional guarantees of their rights as American citizens. And with the Red Scare of the early fifties the lesson was quite clear: Reject any trace of attachment to your ancestral heritage; become a super-patriot, for therein lay the only real alternative to racial discrimination as in the past. By the late fifties and early sixties many had risen to middle-class status and reflected the typical parvenu conservatism of the small homeowner and an irrational fear of intellectual controversy or liberal politics.

evacuation, scholars have blamed the government for falling prey to hysteria and racist pressure groups.[11] But what about the failure of American educators who permitted negative stereotypes to be perpetuated so as to allow the bigots and racists to prey upon the irrational fears of the masses? The educational establishment stands indicted for failing to achieve its prime objective of educating children to become an enlightened, rational citizenry.

Students in elementary and secondary survey courses on social studies and United States history are largely ignorant of significant historical episodes involving Asian Americans—events which are relevant to all Americans. There is little indication that students have been informed of the major role that thousands of Chinese played in the construction of the transcontinental railroad.[12] Moreover, there is no discussion of the overt racism exhibited in the passage of successive federal statutes barring immigration from China or the unannounced invalidation of re-entry permits issued to Chinese who were visiting their homeland—all of which occurred during the decades immediately following the much emphasized ending of slavery.[13]

Nor is there any treatment of the human dimensions, the psychological and linguistic adjustments and everyday anxieties of men, women, and children who were considered incompetent and legally ineligible to testify in courts against white men,[14] to go to the same schools with white children,[15] or to own the farms that they often developed from wastelands through agricultural techniques and seeds which were unknown to most farmers on the western frontier.[16] Where are the tales of overt acts of violence against Chinese frontiersmen and their families—often without

[11] Roger Daniels, "Why It Happened Here," unpublished paper, 1967.

[12] Alexander Saxton, "The Army of Canton in the High Sierra," *Pacific Historical Review* XXXV (1966), 141-152.

[13] In 1882 Congress passed the Chinese Exclusion Act which ended free immigration of Chinese laborers and denied naturalization to Chinese already in this country. The Scott Act of 1888 abruptly invalidated some 20,000 certificates of re-entry granted to Chinese laborers who had left the United States for temporary visits to China. With their permits declared null and void, those Chinese who had left the country were not allowed to return.

[14] In 1885 the testimony of Chinese against Caucasians was prohibited in California.

[15] The San Francisco School Board attempted to place Asian-American students in separate schools in 1906. Upon strong protest from the Japanese government, federal authorities were forced to intervene.

[16] Masakazu Iwata, "The Japanese Immigrants in California Agriculture," *Agricultural History* XXVI, 1 (1962), 25-37. See also W. Jett Lauck, "Japanese

warning in the middle of the night—or the numerous other humiliations and degradations which gave rise to the popular and accurate cliché, "you don't have a Chinaman's chance?"

Few Americans realize that many Asian Americans—particularly the new arrivals and the aged without families to help them—remain completely isolated and remote from both the affluent Asian-American community and the larger society. Because of the early restrictions on Chinese immigration and a history of discrimination which antedated the turn of the century, Chinese communities in America became tightly knit urban concentrations similar to the ghettoes in Europe. Within the Chinatowns the process of acculturation continued at a slow pace and the persistence of traditional family and social relationships and values was strong.[17] By World War II there were signs of demographic movements out of the Chinatowns and greater social mobility within the majority society. But this process was dealt a sharp setback with the Communist conquest of the Chinese mainland in 1949 and the subsequent flow of refugees into overseas Chinese communities. The result has been that the Chinatowns are plagued with overcrowded living spaces, inadequate economic opportunities, and an explosive level of frustration, hopelessness, and despair.[18] The stereotype of the Asian Americans as a successful "model minority" who have "made it" in America is therefore inaccurate and in need of careful re-evaluation.

In United States history and government courses what mention is made of the more recent Japanese-American evacuation and incarceration in America's own concentration camps? What about the legal precedent established by the Supreme Court and the subsequent legislation which provide the foundation for the federal government's construction and continued maintenance of concentration camps for political prisoners even today?[19]

Farmers In Texas—Their Methods Are Being Felt in the Upbuilding of the State," *Texas Magazine* VI (September, 1912), 355-363.

[17] Stanford Lyman, *The Asian in the West* (Reno: University of Nevada, Desert Research Institute, 1971). See pp. 27-32 on "Marriage and the Family Among Chinese Immigrants to America, 1850-1960," pp. 65-80 on "Social Demography of the Chinese and Japanese in the U.S. of America."

[18] Stanley and Derald Sue, "Chinese-American Personality and Mental Health," *Amerasia Journal* I, 2 (July, 1971), 36-49. Kenneth Lamott, "The Awakening of Chinatown," *West Magazine*, January 4, 1970, pp. 6-14.

[19] The Supreme Court of the United States upheld the constitutionality of the Japanese American evacuation on the grounds of "military necessity" and Title II of the Internal Security Act of 1950 provided for the construction and maintenance of

The point is clear. There is much relevance for all Americans in the history of the Asian Americans. Unfortunately, the history of the Asian-American experience in this nation is filled with evidence that democracy and its potential for cultural pluralism is more often given in promises than in practice.

The emphasis of the American educational system on the Western and white Anglo-Saxon Protestant traditions is no longer acceptable to Asian Americans. Unlike their cautious, conservative parents who were raised in an atmosphere of overt racial discrimination, fear of bodily injury, and deprivation of their basic rights as citizens, young Asian Americans are challenging the monocultural ideal of the majority society which in their eyes causes imperialism abroad and the various manifestations of racial inequality at home.[20]

The movement for fundamental changes in our educational process toward the goal of cultural pluralism has great potential as a realistic response to the tensions and frustrations which threaten our society. But if the concept of cultural pluralism is to be advanced with more success than the old melting-pot myth, the Asian Americans cannot continue to be forgotten. The Asian Americans must be acknowledged, analyzed, and incorporated into the curriculum content of educational institutions at all levels of instruction throughout the nation.

Specific improvements include the expansion of foreign language offerings to cover the major languages of Asia, for the world is no longer dominated by Western Europe. The traditional reliance upon French, German, and Spanish no longer suffice at a time when Japan is our chief trading partner and the presence of a powerful mainland China cannot be denied. Courses in world civilizations should reflect the fact that sophisticated cultures existed far to the east of the Fertile Crescent long before the rise of comparable societies in the West. In American history and social studies there must be appropriate treatment of the Asian American contribution to the struggle by peoples from many lands to settle the frontier.

The TTT Program is a hopeful move in this direction. But an expanded focus is essential if the goal of cultural pluralism is to be realized. The absence of a formal presentation on the Asian American experience at the

---

"places of detention." On September 25, 1971, President Nixon announced that he signed the bill to repeal Title II.

[20] Jeffrey Paul Chan, "Let 100 Problems Bloom," *West Magazine*, January 4, 1970, p. 6. Stanford Lyman, "Red Guard on Grant Avenue: The Rise of Youthful Rebellion in Chinatown," in Lyman, op. cit., pp. 99-118. Amy Uyematsu, "The Emergence of Yellow Power in America," *Gidra* I, 7 (October, 1969), 8-11.

recent national Conference on Cultural Pluralism in Education and Teacher Education is but another example of the historical omission of the Asian Americans.[21] At a time when minorities are demanding that our educational system must reflect and serve more honestly and fairly the diversity of subcultures which comprise America, Blacks and Browns may claim "tokenism." But the Asian American can only ask: "I wonder where the yellow went?"

[21] Training the Teacher Trainers, Leadership Training Institute Conference on Education and Teacher Education for Cultural Pluralism, Chicago, Illinois, May 12-14, 1971.

13

THE RISE AND FALL OF ETHNIC STUDIES

VINE DELORIA, JR.

In the last half decade there has been an increasing interest by members of minority groups in the values and historical experiences of their own communities. Several years ago this interest broke forth in the form of protests and demands made by minority students on college and university administrations for the establishment of ethnic studies courses as a regular part of the academic curriculum. Some colleges responded in a positive manner, setting up departments and cluster colleges for work in ethnic studies. Others made a symbolic gesture of having an "awareness" week featuring the national heroes of each group conducting systematic tirades against white culture and values. Others casually ignored the demand altogether by developing remedial programs that alleged to handle the problems of minority groups in new ways.

For the many people who seriously confronted the new idea of emphasizing the experiences of ethnic minorities, ethnic studies meant the possibility of opening up the vision of what America had been and redefining the entire content of social and political thought. And such a task was badly needed. The demand for ethnic studies came as the final gasp of the dying power movements which had suddenly reversed the logic of social movements in 1966 culminating the drive for the development of civil rights which had taken on new forms and energies in 1954.

But few people reckoned with the crash-project conception of ethnic studies that emerged in response to the demand for new academic forms of participation by minority groups. The courses and departments that were put together were by and large anthropology and sociology courses re-warmed and tempered by the contemporary political viewpoints of each group. If ethnic studies resembled anything, it was the frantic ramblings of Henry J. Kaiser's cement shipbuilding program of World War II. Slap things together and hope they last for the duration. Then hope that the duration ends promptly before things are used.

Therefore, the process of developing ethnic studies took on a tradi-tional American mode. The original conception of objective study of community life and values neglected to remember that objective analysis orients the subject matter from production to consumption. And what has been happening in minority communities that have been involved with ethnic studies as a discipline is that they have produced an objectification of their own culture and then proceeded to become consumers of their own products.

Lest the above appear too abstract or vague, we must face a funda-mental philosophical question when we speak of ethnic studies develop-ment. Alvin Toffler and others have pointed out the destructive nature of future thought shaken continually by what Toffler says is "future shock." But the situation has been more serious than that. Nearly a decade ago Daniel Boorstein outlined the nature of the academic dilemma in *The Image*, a book which examined the type of world created by the modern communication media through which we receive our knowledge. Marshall McLuhan followed Boorstein half a decade later with his series of books outlining the thesis that the medium was indeed the message.

Society has undergone a complete transformation in the way that it receives and evaluates its external phenomena in the period since World War II. In this transformation, value judgments and consequent decisions based upon the judgments have unwittingly reversed themselves. We have become a society which lies helpless before the future because our most accurate decisions are not really decisions at all but are gut reactions induced by experiences forced upon us by the media. From these experi-ences we derive our values in the practical sense and then we go through the additional process of re-evaluating the reactions we have against traditional and largely memorized standards of conduct.

We are thus a society without a philosophical base. We stand helpless before a time that bends to accommodate our desire to re-enact our most intense experiences and to negate our most fearful moments. And since the process acts in many instances in defiance of our acknowledgment and out of our control, we, in being selective in our intake, negate a large part of the data which we should be receiving. In this process we have broken society into a number of mutually exclusive masses, each with a constituency deriving its understanding from certain political positions which depend for their validity on charismatic enactment by celebrities who are forced to incarnate images of righteousness and ultimate reality.

In this swirl of nontemporal, or more accurately, multitemporal, and ahistorical happenings, it has proven impossible for ethnic studies to do more than tag along, using traditional techniques of research, compilation, and exposition. The alleged "experiences" are different, therefore, in content only, and not in either point of view or in meaning. What it means to be Black, Chicano, or Indian in American society has not yet been developed. What has been developed is a kind of interpretation of what it means to be semiwhite in this society and colored by the peculiar characteristics of certain groups which have suffered recent oppression within the society, but an oppression tempered and understood in terms of traditional historical interpretations.

A sense of history is badly lacking and it is impossible for people to think in terms of a history that will make sufficient sense to give a validity to the ethnic experience. Once the developing discipline in Black, Chicano, or Indian studies goes beyond the historical period of experiencing the white man in whatever form he first presented himself to the particular group, meaning goes by the boards. If there was a valid historical experience for the Indian before the white man, that would appear to imply that a valid historical experience *after* the white man is needed. If there was a time in Africa prior to the development of the slave trade, then that experience would seem to imply a time when the white man will no longer oppress and enslave.

Again we can take the concept of space, place, and area and ask similar questions which are vital to any meaningful interpretation of experiences. Where do the particular groups exist outside of reservation, barrio, and ghetto? Is Africa, Mexico, or a restored continental America the solution to spatial considerations of ethnic studies? Is it possible for a minority group to create and maintain a sense of countryhood within a nation becoming increasingly more limited in the areas in which it can shift ongoing developments and population centers?

In short, minority groups have discovered history at the precise time when history has ended for the larger majority dominating them politically. Minority groups have discovered space at a time when their white opponents have run out of space. Minority groups have discovered time at a time when time itself is reversible and arbitrarily a function of economics and politics. If the time is not ripe for something, conditions can be developed altering that time and making it suitable for whatever actions are contemplated.

Caught in this situation, the student is at a loss to react to the ethnic studies program in a meaningful sense. Exposition of ideas along traditional channels implies an acceptance of the very values that created the history which he is trying to escape. Content takes on a negative aspect because it has no context within which it can be viewed differently. Incidents of historical importance are casually dismissed as merely another instance of oppression and deceit experienced in everyday life. The student is being driven to accept without question the most nonsensical interpretations of existence because they appear to explain things that in fact have no explanation but merely exist in themselves.

The task of teaching and learning in this whirling mass of facts and values has become virtually impossible to comprehend. The usual solution is to polarize conceivable answers to complex questions so that "good guys" and "bad guys" are identified for the students. Interrelationships of forces wholly above and beyond individual influence become merely the alignment on one side of the fence or the other. The very idea of shifting complexes and points of view to account for the rise and crest of developments becomes an arbitrary exercise of will and not a technique of discovery.

In order to escape this epistemological dilemma both students and teachers have a task as formidable as any faced at any period of history. They must in effect create new logics and new systems of explanation based not so much on discovery of great truths but on emotional satisfaction of the moment. Learning must become the consumption of diverse and conflicting facts and experiences, all of which carry different energy contents, and the conclusions which can be reached by reflection on the period within which the experience occurred.

The field of physics long ago shifted to a logic encompassing alternatives and defining answers according to the systems in which they made most linguistic sense. It quickly became practical and more accurate for scientists to depend upon the Lorenz transformation formulas to translate measured values from one complete and integral system of observation to another. Concepts thus became convenient labels representing processes undertaken during experiments and not ideas valid in and of themselves existing outside the observable universe.

When we talk about law it is equally valid to talk about a system of deprivation set up to oppress certain groups in favor of others. But it is equally valid to consider law as the great civilizing subject which has served to curb racial brutality and discrimination within groups. It is valid to remain within the traditional historical experience of Western European man to examine certain historical periods, but also to connect those experiences to any other periods as a means of uncovering interpretations of either the compared period or the present time.

The traditional Aristotelian logic of either/or, inclusion and exclusion of classes, or the newer both/and logic may be the distinguishing marks of education as we shall come to know it. The Aristotelian logic implies the existence of a real world structure and concerns itself primarily with identities, while the newer logic relates to the incorporation of values and facts within situations, thus speaking ultimately of experienced experiences (if it is possible to speak that way) and not of identities which are assumed to be constant for any sequence.

In spite of the contemporary cry for identity, we do not really mean identity, for we always presume to structure our experiences according to their usefulness in being distinguished from ourselves. When we cry for identity we are seeking the meaning of events in which we are involved. We seek a summary, a sensible summary, of what we have experienced. Or more accurately, what has experienced us. In this sense of the realization of participation we find identity and meaning.

This sense of participation distinguishes students today from all students in the immediate historical past, certainly those students for which the educational system was designed. Students today are experiencing education and are not being educated—at least in the sense that society has been taught to expect them to be educated. At a deeper level than anyone suspects, students are participating in life processes and have for the first time become consumers of educational experience, not simply memorizers of content.

The ethnic student, be he or she at college or primary level, absorbs his or her experiences at about the same rate and in the same manner whether those experiences are in the classroom or the streets. In doing so they demand a new criterion of truth, and spot stalking horses and hypocrisies far better than we do. When teaching we often present them with our beliefs and suffer rejection when they consider them as possible interpretations among a number of possible interpretations.

Until the educational system changes to reflect the world in which we live, we shall not be able to make much headway with minority group students. Much worse, ethnic studies as a discipline will not survive the immediate future because it fails to measure up to traditional measuring devices of effectiveness in transmitting contents of subject areas. Educational systems have been the crutch society has used to "make something" of student raw material. But students today want to "be" and not become something. We have previously defined education and success and other social values as end products opening the doors of life. Today's students have made them simply another timeless, supraspatial, ahistorical alternative of the present.

All too often, however, students have reduced education to a form of entertainment by developing their capacity to experience to an instinctual level. They demand relevancy in the content of courses that, when examined closely, generally means heightened drama in presentation, simplification of issues with judgmental overtones, and teaching methods comparable to the Mount Sinai process of spectacular revelation. The reduction to entertainment may mean that the circle is coming to completion, that they feel the subject has deliberately or unwittingly been reduced to a narrow field unrelated to general consumptive practices in which they are engaged.

Education faces a tremendous challenge and a greater opportunity when confronted with ethnic studies as a discipline and minority group students as co-arbiters of learning processes. The entire field can be judged according to preselected standards which have always occupied center stage in determining the validity of education itself. Or the ethnic field correctly can be considered as the last great opportunity to develop principles of living unfettered by preconceived historical interpretations and cultural imperialism. Academic subjects to be valid and comprehensible must be released from their moorings in Western European views and sent adrift among the societies of men. Unless this is done, the process of education itself will collapse and the human mind will revert to the instinctual prowlings of the animal. All indications of the state of our society are that this condition may already be far on the road to realizing itself, and will replace any conception of civilized man as we have known it.

14

THE U.S. OFFICE OF EDUCATION AND CULTURAL PLURALISM

DON DAVIES AND MIRIAM CLASBY

One of the most exciting and significant things happening in our society today is the growing recognition of the positive value of cultural pluralism. In many different areas of life—academic, professional, artistic—we see signs that the strong tide toward homogeneity that has characterized American society for the past 100 years is ebbing. The rising emphasis on diversity as a national resource has important implications for the direction in which our society moves. These implications are perhaps best seen in our educational system which, in so many ways, reflects, reproduces, and sometimes shapes the larger society.

A multicultural society such as ours faces four broad options for the education of minority groups. The first option defines education as adaptation to the existing majority society and establishes schools which embody the values of the dominant culture. To the degree that members of minority cultures acquire the skills, habits, and characteristics of the dominant culture, they have access to the larger society. As rational as such a pattern may seem from certain perspectives, it is, at root, a form of cultural imperialism, carrying all the attendant evils of domination and exploitation. Members of minority groups are educated to the degree that they are needed in the society.

A logical alternative to this adaptive model is a separatist pattern of

[137

education which encourages cultural isolation. The resulting enclaves inevitably lead to cultural and political fragmentation. Such a pattern can be meaningful only if it is chosen by a group for itself, for a limited period of time.

A third option takes cognizance of the presence of minority groups and introduces accommodations. This education is often described as "meeting special needs" or "beginning where people are." The goal, however, is the same as in the first type—to prepare people to function within the dominant culture. Such an education perpetuates the melting-pot mystique.

The final option also sees education as "beginning where people are," but the goal is to provide what is best for their development. This difference in goal is crucial because it is open ended. It does not prescribe what an individual or group can become. It affirms one value: becoming more human; it operates on one fundamental principle: using one's own potential is a good thing.

This value and this principle are not vague generalities; they are bedrock positions which very clearly indicate a direction for education. They demand, for instance, that education demonstrate a concern for multicultural values. They also point to the primary importance of bilingual studies to enable a minority group member to learn sets of meanings common to the larger society. No longer standing outside, a person can effectively move into the meaning system operating in the larger society and fully hear what others are saying. This inevitably leads to the most important point of all. A valid multicultural education must have an explicit intention to teach for participation in decision-making. A bilingual education can prepare a person to understand what is going on, but there is still need for reinforcement in taking a position. A program for genuine cultural pluralism calls for an education which prepares people to make decisions in matters affecting their lives and to perceive the contradictions in their situation.

A focus on decision-making and on contradictions within individual or group experience clarifies basic questions about where exploitation is, where advantage flows. One of the ironies of our history is that questions about the distribution of advantage within the society are quick to gain the label "subversive." Such questions are fundamental for democracy and essential for its just functioning. If education is to be other than indoctrination and adaptation to the existing system, it must utilize all means to prepare for participation in decision-making.

At a practical level, this means providing a wider range of options within the educational system. There is, fortunately, increasing recognition that our system should offer broad opportunities for people at all ages for where they learn, what they learn, how they learn, and when they learn. There is also growing awareness that the multicultural school is a necessity, that minority representation in school decision-making is essential, that appropriate materials must be available for classroom use.

Much activity toward these ends is already well underway and, directly or indirectly, the Office of Education has played a role in preparing the way for a genuinely pluralistic education. The pioneer efforts of TTT have done much to raise the general level of consciousness of issues and alternatives. The three-year-old Bilingual Education Program represents a major thrust to restructure schools for students in bicultural communities. A number of recent programs—Career Opportunities Program, Urban/Rural School Development Program, Targeting Resources on the Educational Needs of the Disadvantaged (TREND), Teacher Corps—have carefully embodied community participation in decision-making—a component which speaks to the long-range objectives of the schools involved. Reports from the field also indicate that creative personnel in various places have sensed the needs of communities and have already introduced materials and practices to foster cultural pluralism. Federally funded curriculum development projects have produced a range of materials stressing a problem-orientation which enables students to formulate responses in terms of their own experiences and styles, strengths and abilities. Some of these specifically focus on diversity within a classroom, utilizing it as a resource for richer and deeper insight.

All this is, of course, just a beginning and there is need for much more work. If education is to encourage a pluralistic society, the Office of Education, state departments of education, individual school systems, teachers, and teacher trainers will have to develop overall strategies for their efforts, integrating discrete activities in a clear conceptual framework. Because such an education challenges existing styles, it will arouse controversy. Careful attention, therefore, must be given to clarifying objectives and validating means. The task is enormous and, by its nature, on-going.

The value shift from an emphasis on homogeneity to a recognition of diversity as a national resource did not begin in the classrooms and it will not end there. But schools can play a central role in the process of its development. The public school helped to create and sustain the melting pot of the nineteenth and twentieth centuries. The public school today, by demonstrating a concern for cultural values, by encouraging bilingual education, and by preparing for participation can be a vital instrument in establishing the attitudes and information necessary for the change to a justly pluralistic society.

15

THE MELTING – POT THEORY:
DEMISE OF EUPHEMISM

WILLIAM L. SMITH

An article by an English professor recently appeared in a Washington newspaper. It had to do with the proliferation of euphemisms. Hardly any profession or institution has failed to succumb to what the author called "costume jewelry" semantics. Here are some examples: Undertakers employ "grief counselors." Looking for a job becomes "plotting a career strategy." If a project runs over its budget, you have a "suboptimal cost profile." And "anticipatory communism" is what a square would call stealing. The example I liked best quoted the chief of police of a large city. Responding to an allegation that certain members of his department were involved in corruption, he admitted that the charge was "potentially factual." The point of the article was that our reluctance to call a rose by its name seems to verge on the pathological.

If we have become proficient in evasive vocabulary, it may well be that it is because we have had long years of practice. For instance, I would match the nineteenth century term "melting pot" against any of the circumlocutions that the most skilled modern-day Madison Avenue practitioner could turn out. It was a term that was "potentially factual" for it described what was essentially a process for recycling junk. It implied that the broken down and worthless trash from across the seas—immigrants from all but the Anglo-Saxon world—could be poured into a giant cauldron and under extreme heat and pressure somehow be molded into a shiny new product, something typically American that we could proudly label "Made in the U.S.A."

In recent years, the melting-pot theory has fallen into disrepute, but the message has not reached all segments of society and, hence, it has not reached all of our schools. How many Indian and Black and Chicano and Puerto Rican and Oriental children are still in classrooms where teachers are stirring or crushing or pressing them into something other than what they are? How many schools are still in the service of a uniculture where assimilation into that culture is rewarded by the right to wear a white hat and where those who fail to earn that distinction are labeled bad guys?

For many teachers, and indeed for all school personnel including superintendents, the concept of a multicultural society is difficult to grasp. That is understandable. It betrays the tenets by which they have been living. Most people, no matter what their credentials, have never known the good side of living in a multicultural world. Nothing in what they have learned—history from textbooks; lifestyle from advertising; cultural biases from movies, employment institutions, and law enforcement agencies; or teaching techniques from colleges and universities—has prepared them for understanding or living in a pluralistic society.

This is still a cowboy and Indian world where the good guys—whether they are following the political trail or riding into the sunset—wear white skins under their white hats, speak standard English (unless it is a cowboy drawl), and, most important of all, never lose a fight. There is still a strong tradition that equates Anglo-American origin and Anglo-American ways with virtue, with goodness, even with political purity. For many, breaking with such a strong tradition may be painful, but it is not pardonable. It must be done and I believe it can be done. Three hundred years of ethnic minority experiences, though bitter, must not be blotted from time, for they helped to shape the identities of both minority and majority groups.

Some weak starts have been made in the schools in moving toward a multicultural approach, but not always for the right reasons. The inclusion of minority studies has been used as a strategy by many school administrators to defuse protest and relieve anticipated pressures. This has been a stopgap measure, a finger stuck in the dike. Real issues have not been dealt with and they won't be until teachers know how to use sensitive material and fuse it with the ongoing curriculum. Little progress will be made until teachers feel secure in handling these materials in all classrooms, those with minority children and those without. Nothing significant is likely to take place until teachers have come to know and accept themselves and until they come to know and accept the kids with whom they work and have influence.

When the state boards of education expressed the view that minority curricula were extraneous unless a large portion of the school population consisted of minorities, they were negating the entire purpose of education. In today's world, the goal of education must be to develop individuals who are open to change, who are flexible and adaptive and receptive. This means introducing the student to a variety of lifestyles, not superficially, but in depth. Students of all races must study the richness of America's multicultural heritage. Canada is already officially promoting ethnic diversity. There is no model Canadian citizen.

All of what I am advocating can be defined simply as a humanistic approach to education. Teachers of the handicapped pinpoint it this way: The "different" child is not an "inferior" child. All teachers need to adopt that same creed and become sensitive to the learning needs and abilities, the personal interests and motivations, and the ethnic and cultural differences that set one child apart from another.

Programs developed under the Education Professions Development Act have already had a marked impact on broadening the capabilities and sensitivities of teachers and other educational personnel. We have striven to extend the range of human variability. In doing so, we have also broadened the range of differences, acceptable pupil behavior, and performance. For example, the bilingual program has introduced teachers to the concept that Spanish-speaking and Indian children can learn as well as any others once they are allowed to communicate in their own language. When given the opportunity to learn subject matter in their native tongue while learning English in other classes, marked progress has been noted. Educators exposed to such new concepts generally agree that children should not be boxed into such categories as "discipline problem," "slow learner," or "physically impaired," but should be allowed to develop as individuals. The humanistic approach becomes increasingly important as more young teachers, finding fewer job opportunities in the suburbs, begin their careers in low-income and culturally mixed neighborhoods.

Implicit in the humanistic approach is an individualized approach requiring more options in the classroom, more specialized skills and confidence on the part of the teacher, and more diversified curriculum materials and teaching aides than are available in most traditional educational settings.

No matter what you call it—the multicultural, the pluralistic, or the humanistic approach—only a very few fortunate individuals are born with it. A heavy burden for transmitting the required skills and attitudes rests with teacher training institutions, and they have not distinguished themselves in this area. If colleges and universities are to function effectively, they must turn out personnel capable of (1) identifying, through observation and testing, the child with special problems and needs; (2) diagnosing those problems and needs accurately; and (3) developing from a range of behavioral objectives and teaching techniques an individual program that will help the child overcome or at least remediate his difficulties. For teachers already in the schools and lacking those skills, retraining programs have been supported by the Bureau of Educational Personnel Development (now renamed the National Center for the Improvement of Educational Systems).

The identification-diagnostic-prescriptive skills cannot be limited to the cognitive realm. Until teachers are trained to work in the area of human relationships as well as in teaching subject matter, until they can enter the affective realm, the transition to cultural pluralism will remain elusive. Only when the teacher, along with his students, can answer the ontological questions—where he came from and who he is and where he is going—can they move forward to share with others and learn from others. Until such a time, a truly pluralistic society remains another euphemism, an exercise in "costume jewelry" semantics, something only "potentially factual."

16

PLURALISM AND CULTURAL PLURALISM IN THE TRAINING THE TEACHER TRAINERS PROGRAM

MARY JANE SMALLEY

The emergence of cultural pluralism as a central concern of the Training the Teacher Trainers program is not surprising. When the TTT began in December, 1967, there was not an explicit commitment to the concept of cultural pluralism and its implementation in all projects. There was, however, insistence upon another kind of equity basic to teacher training: "decisional" pluralism among all the groups and agencies affected by or affecting the training that teachers receive. It was this sense of equity which, by the course of its development, made inevitable the emergence of the demand for cultural pluralism which was first noted in early 1970.

The TTT program posed a new and difficult question: Who has the expertise needed to train the teacher trainers who in turn are responsible for both preservice and inservice education of teachers for the nation's schools? Most especially, who can train teachers for work in the schools in those distressed, low-income areas where the inadequacies of schooling are most evident? From the beginning, the answer was clear that no one alone had that expertise, although in fact there have always been people whose life work it is—to a large extent unrecognized or unknown to them!—to train the trainers of teachers. The TTT program proposed a strategy of pluralistic decision-making in all matters related to teacher education. This strategy brought into coalition the university—both its liberal arts and teacher education colleges—the schools, and the communities served by those institutions. The proposed coalition—a sharing of power by sharing the making of decisions—meant in fact that both kinds of institutions and the individuals in them would share the planning and implementation of training programs for teachers and, even more importantly, would share responsibility in the assessment of their success and failure.

This venture in educational pluralism, which came to be known as "parity," was described in a number of ways. To some people it was an attempt to "open the system," for they believe that education in the United States—albeit constitutionally a local matter and at the higher education level characterized by extreme decentralization—is to a great extent a closed system, a closed system in important ways to the minorities as teachers and students, a system which at all levels classifies and labels children and in fact maintains the socioeconomic status quo, despite its lesser role of social leveler and promoter of upward mobility. This pursuit of pluralism was also viewed in early TTT documents as an attempt to change the relationships of "producers" and "consumers" in the educational enterprise. The enforced involvement of the latter with the former in TTT decision-making has challenged the once-unchallengeable authority of the institution of higher education and has created new, powerful roles for the consumers. The definitions of producer and consumer have since been broadened. Originally the schools were thought of simply as consumers of the university's products, even as the communities seemed to be consumers of what the schools produced.

The first group to challenge this concept and identify itself as a consumer, separate and with its own right to be heard, was the students: post-doctoral fellows, graduate students, undergraduates, high school and even junior high school students. In varying ways these individuals demanded a voice and place alongside the other constituencies in the TTT projects. Further, the university began to see itself more clearly as a consumer in relation to the schools; the schools viewed themselves in a consumer relationship to the parents; and, finally, the community recognized its own various consumer roles: as a largely unorganized group relating broadly to the educational system, and individually, as parents, the consumers of specific output from the TTT and other classrooms.

This pluralistic strategy produced a broader, more eclectic view of training than had ever been known before, characterized by frequent moving of people from one institution to another one where they were obliged to assume new roles and relate in new and different ways to other teachers and learners. For example, the experience of a graduate professor of English teaching in a first-grade classroom in a team with his graduate students, master teachers, student teachers, and community aides constitutes a rare, revealing, and sometimes chastening kind of training, especially for one who might not have visited an elementary school classroom in the previous twenty years. This example has many corollaries: community personnel on university admissions committees, master teachers as clinical professors, school supervisors as aides in community agencies. Such training is not easy for those who plan and direct it nor for those who undergo it. It marked a radical departure from usual practice both in the target group of trainees and in the content of the training. It was pluralistic and an invitation to still other manifestations of pluralism.

Clearly, cultural pluralism became an issue in TTT projects as a result of this widening of participation in educational programming, and especially from the TTT's heavy involvement of persons from the underrepresented minorities and its major focus on the education of these groups. This kind of pluralism manifests itself in bilingual-bicultural education, ethnic studies, and above all in the recruitment and training of members of these groups for positions as teachers, administrators, linguists, sociologists, historians, etc. Except for bilingual-bicultural education, however, these activities are essentially efforts toward the achievement of social justice, i.e., fairness and a fair share for everyone. This is cultural pluralism only in a limited sense, because it is basically assimilative in orientation. It does not, however, negate and indeed may be a preliminary step toward cultural pluralism in its fuller sense: the right not to assimilate and still know fairness and a fair share for everyone.

The commitment of the TTT program to open discussion of cultural pluralism was expressed most directly in the conference held in Chicago in May, 1971. Again there was no prescription. Cultural pluralism was not defined in advance nor was there any judgment made of the appropriateness—even to the stated theme of the conference—of presentations by the speakers, reactors, group leaders, or other participants. As a result, some of the presentations have little apparent pertinence to that theme, but the concept was explored in an unlimited variety of ways, and those multiple points of view find expression in the present publication.

What does cultural pluralism mean then in the TTT context? It is, first of all, more than the collection of certain activities which exemplify cultural pluralism in certain projects, just as the TTT Program is more than the sum of its thirty or forty projects. It is more than the conference of which this book is the record. The process which produced the conference is representative of the ability of a program organized as the TTT was—on the basis of a new concept of the institutions and individuals who should be involved in educational planning—to surface significant issues, explore them, and most importantly place them in the rhetoric and on the agenda of American education.

APPENDIX A. STATEMENT BY THE STEERING COMMITTEE OF THE NATIONAL COALITION FOR CULTURAL PLURALISM[1]

America has long been a country whose uniqueness and vitality have resulted in large part from its human diversity. However, among all the resources formerly and currently used to insure physical and social progress for this nation, the human resource with its myriad ethnic, cultural, and racial varieties has not been used to its fullest advantage. As a result, the American image that has been delineated by its governmental, corporate, and social structures has not truly reflected the cultural diversity of its people.

There should be no doubt in anyone's mind that America is now engaged in an internal social revolution that will thoroughly test her national policies and attitudes regarding human differences. This revolution manifests itself in many ways, through many movements. Blacks, Spanish Americans, women, college students, elderly people, etc., are all finding themselves victimized by technological and social systems which look upon significant differences among people as unhealthy and inefficient. But, whether the society likes it or not, many individuals and groups will never be able to "melt" into the American "pot." And it is these groups who are now gearing themselves up to be more self-determining about their own destinies. For them it is a simple matter of survival in America.

In the future, surviving in America will of necessity be the major concern of every citizen, regardless of his wealth, heritage, race, sex, or age. This has already been made abundantly clear by the developing crisis in ecology. The national concern over pollution, overpopulation, etc., will probably be solved through our technological expertise. But the social crisis facing this country will require a different solution concept, one which will provide unity with diversity where the emphasis is on a shared concern for creating and maintaining a multicultural environment.

[1]See page 6.

The concept of cultural pluralism, therefore, must be the perspective used by the different social groups in their attempt to survive as independent, yet interdependent, segments of this society. Pluralism lifts up the necessary and creative tension between similarity and difference. It strongly endorses standards of variety, authentic options, diverse centers of power, and self-direction.

It is the institutions of our society which provide the supports for some individual and group attitudes, values, and standards which, when applied, are clearly discriminatory against others. It is these same institutions which can reverse many of the current social trends by establishing supports for a culturally pluralistic society—where everyone recognizes that no single set of values and standards is sufficient to inspire the full range of human possibilities.

The creation of a truly multicultural society will not happen automatically. There must be established a plan of action, a leadership, and a cadre of supporters that will effectively implement the concept of cultural pluralism throughout the length and breadth of every community in America. Institutions, groups, and individuals must be actively engaged in working toward at least three goals, which are:

1. The elimination of all structural supports for oppressive and racist practices by individuals, groups, and institutions.
2. The dispersal of "power" among groups and within institutions on the basis of cultural, social, racial, sexual, and economic parity.
3. The establishment and promotion of collaboration as the best mechanism for enabling culturally independent groups to function cooperatively within a multicultural environment.

The accomplishment of these and other goals can be facilitated only through a national effort. Therefore, the emergence of the National Coalition for Cultural Pluralism is an important first step in the right direction.

Widespread support and private contributions will be sought in order to implement a more specific delineation of purpose, structure, and incorporation.

APPENDIX B. CONFERENCE PERSONNEL

Chairman and Reactors[1]

Aquino-Bermudez, Federico
Department of Urban Studies
City College (City University of
New York)
New York, New York 10031

Arnez, Nancy
Director, Center for Inner City
Studies
Northeastern Illinois State College
700 East Oakland Blvd.
Chicago, Illinois 60625

Certa, Maria
Member, Chicago Board of
Education
228 North LaSalle Street
Chicago, Illinois 60601

Flores, Solomon
Professor of Education
University of Maryland
College Park, Maryland 20742

Fox, Sylvia
Director, Aspira Inc. of Illinois
767 North Milwaukee Avenue
Chicago, Illinois 60622

Gonzales, Nell
Director, Bilingual Project
Chicago Public Schools
228 North LaSalle Street
Chicago, Illinois 60601

Harris, LaDonna
1820 Jefferson Place N.W.
Washington, D.C. 20036

Jackson, Gene
Palomar Community College
San Marcos, California 92069

Jones, J. B.
Director, TTT Project
Professor of Psychology
Texas Southern University
3201 Wheeler
Houston, Texas 77004

Louie, James
Chairman, Berkeley Asian American Education Task Force
1122 Keeler Avenue
Berkeley, California 94708

MacCalla, Thomas
U.S. International University
8655 Pommerado Road
San Diego, California 92124

Mathew, Alfredo
Superintendent District 3
New York City Public Schools
New York, New York 10025

McClelland, L. K.
Woodlawn Organization
1135 East 63 Street
Chicago, Illinois 60637

McKnight, John L.
Assistant Director, Urban Affairs
Center
Northwestern University
Evanston, Illinois 60201

---

[1] Since the presenters' papers are published in this volume and their biographies appear on pages ix-xv, *The Contributors*, their names have been omitted from this list.

Ney, James
Arizona State University
Tempe, Arizona 85281

Salmeron, Rudolph
5100 West Oakdale Avenue
Chicago, Illinois 60641

U.S. Office of Education

Bigelow, Donald N.
Director, Division of College
  Programs
Bureau of Educational Personnel
  Development

Davies, Don
Deputy Commissioner for Develop-
  ment
Office of Education

Foster, Charles R.
Education Program Specialist
TTT Branch, Division of College
  Programs
Bureau of Educational Personnel
  Development

Radcliffe, Shirley
Education Program Specialist
TTT Branch, Division of College
  Programs
Bureau of Educational Personnel
  Development

Reed, Charles R.
Education Program Specialist
TTT Branch, Division of College
  Programs
Bureau of Educational Personnel
  Development

Schmieder, Allen A.
Head of Task Force '72
Bureau of Educational Personnel
  Development

Smalley, Mary Jane
Chief, TTT Branch, Division of
  College Programs
Bureau of Educational Personnel
  Development

Smith, William L.
Associate Commissioner
Bureau of Educational Personnel
  Development

Tinsman, Stewart
Acting Director, Division of
  College Programs
Bureau of Educational Personnel
  Development

Tuttle, Donald R.
Education Program Specialist
TTT Branch, Division of College
  Programs
Bureau of Educational Personnel
  Development

APPENDIX C. MAJOR CONFERENCE
RECOMMENDATIONS

The main focus of the Conference on Education and Teacher Education for Cultural Pluralism was on developing suggestions for action to make cultural pluralism a central factor in American education. After the conference, these suggestions were to be forwarded to appropriate persons and organizations for their reaction and action. As indicated in the description of the conference which appears in Chapter 1 of this report, maximum time was allocated to meetings of discussion groups that were small enough to come to grips effectively with the task of formulating recommendations. There were eight such groups, each of which included representatives from the community, school, liberal arts, and teacher education sectors of the TTT projects that participated in the conference. Altogether, more than 100 recommendations resulted from the work of these groups.

As could be expected, a number of important ideas were treated by more than one group so that there was some repetition from group to group in the suggestions that emerged. A committee of the TTT LTI was given the task of studying the original recommendations, combining those that dealt with a common idea, and determining where each recommendation should be forwarded for action. When the committee had completed its work, the number of recommendations had been reduced to sixty-seven without losing any of the suggestions contained in the original list. Each of the sixty-seven recommendations was then forwarded by the director of TTT LTI to the place or places that the committee had decided could most appropriately take action on it. That the recommendations have indeed stimulated widespread concern for cultural pluralism in education is indicated by the correspondence which has ensued between the director of TTT LTI and many of the persons and organizations to whom recommendations were sent. Further activities to capitalize on this concern are now under way.

In the course of its work, the TTT LTI committee identified thirty-one major recommendations that it considered to be focused directly on some aspect of cultural pluralism, while the remainder dealt with matters that were related to schools and to teacher education in a more general way. The list which follows presents the thirty-one major recommendations. The order in which they are given is not to be taken as suggesting their order of importance. Rather, it is the result of the committee's efforts to make broad groupings of the major suggestions about culturally pluralistic education that emerged from the conference.

1. Cultural pluralism should be recognized in the selection of personnel for decision-making bodies in all federal education programs so that minority communities will have a policy role in such programs. This principle should be applied at all levels of a program, from top-level positions in the U.S. Office of Education (USOE) to the personnel of individual projects, and at the state and local levels. Particular communities that are involved in a specific program should be represented in the decision-making bodies of that program. That is, no group should have the right to assume representation for another minority community in determining policy for the program.

2. All learning materials that are used in school instruction—audiovisual materials, periodicals, etc., as well as textbooks—should be accurately representative of ethnic minorities so as to implement the concept of cultural pluralism. A condition for any school district to receive federal funds of any kind should be that it will utilize only materials that meet this criterion. Publishing companies which produce materials that do not meet this criterion should be boycotted.

3. A clearinghouse for the dissemination of culturally pluralistic materials and teaching strategies that are being used in the various TTT projects should be established by the national director of the TTT program.

4. A pool of consultants on culturally pluralistic learning materials should be established, with its members drawn from the community, school, and higher education sectors of TTT. The services of these consultants should be available to TTT projects for the development of culturally pluralistic materials.

5. The USOE program officer of the TTT program should take the lead in seeking sources for funds and other assistance to have culturally pluralistic materials prepared for publication by minority groups and to have these materials promoted so they become available for use in the schools.

6. Standardized tests should be used only for purposes of instructional diagnosis and improvement of individual children, not as a basis for

excluding children from normal educational experiences. In all such testing, the tester must speak the language of the child and the test(s) should be selected with consideration for the cultural setting in which the child has grown. The tests must be administered and interpreted in terms of the child's background.

7. The arts should be recognized and utilized as a fundamental tool for understanding and developing the concept of cultural pluralism.

8. The USOE, state education departments, and/or other educational agencies should develop a screening process that local schools can apply to determine that teachers, administrators, and other educational personnel who are newly employed, or who are to receive tenure, salary increment, or other advancement, have the understanding of cultural pluralism, the sensitivity, and the commitment required to implement improved education for children of all ethnic groups.

9. School systems and universities should cooperate to provide training programs for educational personnel who need additional experiences in the area of cultural pluralism. School administrators, for example, should receive training in the areas of institutional management, organizational behavior, and theories of individual and societal development.

10. The need for multicultural staffing, particularly in positions of power such as those of administrators or program coordinators, should be recognized in appointments and promotions of professional personnel in school systems and universities.

11. State certification agencies should develop more creative and flexible criteria for certifying teachers and other educational personnel, recognizing such factors as relevant life experience and a bilingual, bicultural background. The new criteria should include an emphasis on understanding the concept of cultural pluralism and on developing commitment to seeking innovative approaches for implementing this concept. They should encourage teacher education institutions to redesign their programs to stress the development of this understanding and commitment in students through such approaches as the use of community resources (both people and physical facilities), provision for internship in community settings, and inclusion of ethnic studies in the curriculum of future teachers.

12. Certification criteria for educational personnel in programs of bilingual education should include evidence of experience in and commitment to the community (Spanish, Chinese, etc.) which the particular program is to serve.

13. Minority group communities should have parity, along with the

university and the school district, in program planning and operation of TTT projects. Students who are representative of the community to which the project is directed should be included as a component of parity. The selection of community representatives and of project personnel from the community should be made by organized community groups, and people from the community should receive pay for the services they render that is equal to the pay given to professional (credentialed) personnel of the project.

14. Each project should maintain an active policy-making board in which there is parity among community, school, and university. This board should be provided with resources for monthly review of project operations, with immediate feedback and program modification based on the board's recommendations.

15. To insure that the community component of TTT has real authority at the decision-making level, project funds should go directly to community groups, which may then make contracts with the universities and appropriate agencies.

16. An evaluation (audit) of all TTT projects should be made to ensure that objectives are being met, and the results should be made public. Parents, college students, professional groups, and community leaders should participate in the evaluation.

17. School systems should be decentralized so that schools will be controlled by a community body representative of the school's student population, thus giving minority groups power over the educational institutions of their children and enabling local communities to encourage publishing companies to produce the types of materials that their children can use to full advantage.

18. To facilitate communication between university and community, and to insure that the community has a voice in determining directions of development within the university, community people should be placed on the governing board and major policy-making committees of the university. There should also be a definite structure for flow of information between community and university, with mutual agreement on such points as the nature of information that should be exchanged and how it will be assembled.

19. The USOE should recognize its accountability by making public its decisions regarding project selection (and refusals) and the choice of project administrators in federally funded programs such as TTT. Projects that are funded should contain a component that is specially related to

problems and issues related to cultural pluralism and should present evidence of a commitment to the concept of cultural pluralism.

20. University programs for the preparation of teachers should be structured so as to provide both students and faculty with extensive experiences in the schools and in the organizations and agencies of the communities that are served by the schools. To insure integration of the field experiences into all parts of the program, faculty members who are not involved directly in these experiences should engage in in-service observations, seminars, and workshops focused on the schools and their communities. The various cultural groups in these communities should help to plan and implement the orientation of students and faculty to their particular cultures. To facilitate both the input from the community and the integration of the field experiences into more theoretical aspects of the teacher training program, many activities that traditionally have been conducted on campus should take place in school and community settings. One way of implementing this goal would be to have university faculty members given dual appointments in the university and the local school.

21. The university should establish centers for the study of contemporary social questions and issues, such as those associated with the implementation of cultural pluralism. In such centers, faculty from various disciplines as well as experts not associated with the university should be brought together to focus on the development of effective approaches and institutions for dealing with these questions and issues.

22. The USOE and other appropriate agencies should establish programs for the preparation of university faculty and for research in the various fields of ethnic studies, including research on the cognitive structure of minority cultures. Ethnic colleges should be established where feasible and advisable for the training of experts in these fields. One dimension of such programs should be the development of international cultural exchange as appropriate to the particular field of focus, e.g., with Spanish-speaking countries in the case of ethnic studies focused on Puerto Rican and Mexican-American cultures or with East European countries in the case of Slavic studies.

23. Strong ethnic studies programs should be established in colleges and universities, with adequate facilities and financial support, and should be so oriented as to serve nonminority students as well as others. Ethnic studies should be attached to some marketable skills program. Some work in ethnic studies should be required of all prospective teachers. The

group(s) upon which such an ethnic studies program is focused should be in control of the program.

24. The university must give recognition and credit toward professional advancement to all of those who implement action programs as they do to those who publish.

25. Every high school graduate should have the opportunity for higher education. To this end, colleges and universities should adopt the open enrolment admission policy. In addition, community junior colleges, where high school graduates who do not wish to attend a four-year college can obtain training in a skill, should be established where they do not already exist, and graduates of a junior college who wish to continue their education should be guaranteed admission into senior colleges.

26. The university should be a source of technical assistance that will enable the community to institutionalize its knowledge and capabilities as a marketable commodity and to make effective use of channels for change. Specifically, federally funded projects should allocate money to providing such technical assistance to the community.

27. The so-called general curriculum track should be eliminated from secondary school programs and alternatives should be developed to provide minority group students with training leading either to a skilled craft or successful university study. Universities should cooperate with school systems and communities in developing more effective academic courses and more relevant occupational training in the schools.

28. Bilingualism should be recognized as an asset, not a liability, and school programs should be structured to enable bilingual students to capitalize on this asset. For example, curriculum experiences should be developed to maximize the advantages of a bilingual, bicultural background.

29. In bilingual programs, the role of the second language should be clarified and defined at all levels of instruction.

30. Bilingual, bicultural paraprofessionals recruited from the community should be recognized as essential components of improved education for bilingual, bicultural children of the various ethnic groups; consequently universities and school districts should cooperate to provide adequate training programs for such community people.

31. Each community should define the credentials for its teachers.

APPENDIX D. ANNOTATED
BIBLIOGRAPHY OF FILMS

Films and television are the pervasive and eloquent medium of today. Perhaps no other mode provides such opportunities for stimulating the interchange of attitudes, opinions, and responses. It becomes evident that there are several levels of communication present in most screen experiences:

- verbal communication between persons in the film;
- nonverbal communication between persons in the film;
- environmental communication (the setting in which the persons are found);
- sound track other than voice (special effects, music, and environmental sound);
- the selected images that the frame of the camera has included; and the implication of the images absent;
- the total, verbal, nonverbal, and psychological aspect of the film communicated to the audience.

Our purpose in offering this film program was to provide new directions and approaches for reaching an understanding of the lives of the people portrayed, including their environmental conditions, their hopes, their despairs, their aspirations, their frustrations, their weaknesses, and their strengths. The rationale for these approaches is discussed more fully by Dr. Anthony W. Hodgkinson in Part II of this appendix.

The films that were selected for the conference are listed in the following pages and were chosen by a previewing committee which was engaged by the Northeast TTT Cluster and which met at Hunter College, New York, on March 26 and 27, 1971, to make its selections.[1] Based on

[1] The members of the committee were William Byers (Chairman), Worcester Consortium for Higher Education, Screen Study Center, Worcester, Massachusetts; Federico Aquino-Bermudez, Department of Urban and Ethnic Studies, City College of the City University of New York (CUNY), New York, N.Y. (March 27 session only); Patricia Hill, teacher, St. Joseph's School, Roxbury, Massachusetts; Mrs. Mifaunwy Shunatona Hines, Secretary, American Indian Community House, Inc.,

the reactions of the previewers, William Byers and Anthony Hodgkinson prepared the program at the direction of Mrs. Sylvia Bernstein, Administrative Director, Northeast TTT Cluster.

The films that were previewed by no means exhausted available resources. Initial reference may be made to Educational Film Library Association, 17 West 60th Street, New York, N.Y. 10023, and to "Ethnic Studies and Audio-visual Media: a Listing and Discussion," by Harold A. Layer, an Occasional Paper from ERIC at Stanford University, available from ERIC Clearinghouse on Educational Media and Technology at the Institute for Communication Research, Stanford University, Stanford, California 94305.

Part I: A Selected List of Films for Culturally Pluralistic Education

An American Girl (B.[2]   b/w   28 min.)
An adolescent non-Jewish white girl purposefully identifies herself as being Jewish in order to test the democratic traditions in which she has been reared. She exposes her experiences with anti-Semitism and explores the problem by reading her diary at a P.T.A. meeting.

A Time For Burning (C.   b/w   58 min.)
Based on the suggested merger of two Midwestern Lutheran Church parishes, one white and one Negro, this film explores the attempts to overcome prejudices and misunderstandings.

How Come When It's Thundering—You Don't See the Moon?
(B.   color   13 min.)
A high-school-aged Harlem youth views his world through drawings, paintings, and school. Deals with what children are, what they can be, and must be helped to become.

New York, N.Y.; Anthony Hodgkinson, Associate Professor of Screen Education, Worcester Consortium for Higher Education, Worcester, Massachusetts; Eduardo Irlanda, Department of Urban and Ethnic Studies, City College, CUNY, New York, N.Y. (March 26 session only); Rita Murray, Community Representative, Hartford TTT Center, Hartford, Connecticut; Wayne Proudfoot, Department of Religious Studies, Fordham University, New York, N.Y.; Lawrence Waxberg, Student, Brooklyn College, CUNY, Brooklyn, New York.

[2] See pages 164-165 for Distributor Code.

Huelga! (A.D.F.   color   50 min.)
The struggles of C. Chavez to organize the grape pickers into a union and to gain better working and living conditions.

Maria of the Pueblos (C.C.   color   15 min.)
Depicts the life of Maria Martinez, whose rediscovery of the long-forgotten secret process for creating iridescent black pottery helped lift her village out of poverty. The purpose of the film is to encourage an understanding and appreciation of the culture, philosophy, art, and economic condition of the North American Indians, particularly the Pueblo Indians of San Ildefonso, New Mexico.

My Own Yard to Play In (E.C.   b/w   10 min.)
A lyrical social documentary revealing the fascinating inventive world of children at play, offering insights into urban problems. (Filmed in New York.)

No Place to Go (C.F.W.C.   b/w   18 min.)
What happens to the living patterns of a neighborhood when urban renewal comes to the area? What do the people do? What are their problems, frustrations? Where do they go? This film looks at these questions in the context of urban renewal in the area of Lincoln Center in New York.

North American Indian (C.   color   90 min.)
Part 1. "Treaties Made—Treaties Broken"
   Only in the last few years have White North Americans begun to admit that they have broken treaties made with the North American Indians. This film focuses upon the Indians of Washington State and the Treaty of Medicine Creek and the abrogation of that treaty by the State of Washington.
Part 2. "How the West Was Won . . . and Honor Lost"
   This film is history . . . from the landing of Columbus through the signing of treaties by the founding fathers of the United States; the breaking of those treaties; the forced marches of the "Indian Removal"; the genocidal "victory" of the U.S. Seventh Cavalry in the Battle of Wounded Knee. The inevitable question: "Where is honor in this history?"
Part 3. "Lament of the Reservation"
   The Sioux of South Dakota were herded onto reservations in the

Badlands of South Dakota. Within the thousands of acres of near-worthless land existed some arable land that was either distributed in parcels too small and too widely dispersed to be usable, or was taken over by white farmers and ranchers. Extreme poverty, high infant mortality, unemployment nearing 65 percent at times breeds in adolescents and adults a despair leading to the "no-solutions" of suicide. The question: "What price for the right of an Indian to remain as Indian?"

Nothing But a Man (B.   b/w   92 min.)
The personal struggle of a Southern Negro railway worker, and his marriage to the school-teaching daughter of the Negro preacher. The couple's attempts to build a life in a society hostile to them both.

Now That the Buffalo Has Gone (D.F.L.   color   6 min.)
A rapid, short history of the destruction of both the Plains ecology and the economy of the Plains Indian by the coming of the white man.

16 in Webster Groves (E.C.   b/w   47 min.)
A biting indictment of affluent suburbia. T.V. journalism at its best; exposes a large segment of society . . . smug, complacent, insulated against our seething social problems.

Span/Eng the Bilingual Gap (B.V.S.D.   color   30 min.)
This film relates the experiences of a Mexican-American boy. It deals with the awakening consciousness of Chicano problems on the part of the Anglo community.

Still a Brother: Inside the Negro Middle Class
(D.F.L.   b/w   90 min.)
An exploration of the crises faced by the Negro middle class. Different points of view are presented by prominent persons.

Streets of Greenwood (B.   b/w   20 min.)
The conflict of attitudes about Negro voting rights; documentation of 1964 voter registration drives in Mississippi and the organization of the Mississippi Freedom Democratic Party. The Negro community's struggle for freedom is contrasted with the white community's efforts to maintain the status quo.

Subversion (F.W.   color   30 min.)
The narrated personal experiences and tragic images of the Japanese
Americans "detained" during World War II in the now infamous camps.
The film reveals the effects of fear and racism on three generations in this
strange period of history.

The Ballad of Crowfoot (D.F.L.   b/w   10 min.)
A reflection of the attitudes, problems, and traditions of some American
Indians.

The Exiles (C.   b/w   72 min.)
A documentary of the problems faced by American Indians living in urban
areas, especially the conflict of cultures.

The Gorilla (C.F.W.C.   color   10 min.)
A Puerto Rican adolescent boy caught up in social struggles.

The Long Walk (F.W.   color   60 min.)
In 1864 Kit Carson marched the Navajo Indians through 300 miles of
snow to their "new home" on a reservation. The effects took their toll on
the Indian way of life and culture, but now, through their own efforts,
they are regaining their heritage and self-respect in their own schools,
teaching their own language as well as the American way of life.

The Tenement (M.M.M.   b/w   40 min.)
This documentary is an absorbing indictment of poverty that speaks
through the lips of the people caught within the social disease of ghetto
life. Yet, the film has captured the spark of hope and strength that remains
within the lives of the people of Chicago's South Ellis Avenue tenement
building that is the focal point for the film.

12-12-42 (M.M.M.   color   11 min.)
A satirical portrait of a national type through an interview with a young
woman whose simplistic outlook on life is in contrast with visuals of
battlefield horror and poverty.

You Are on Indian Land (C.   b/w   37 min.)
Blockade of the International Bridge between the United States and
Canada. This film, made by Mike Mitchell, member of the Company of

Young Canadians' Indian Film Crew, views the organization of the non-violent protest by the Indians to gain the cooperation of the Canadian and the United States governments in honoring a treaty of 1794 granting Indian rights to duty-free passage over the border.

Walkout Woodlake (C.F.W.C.   color   5 min.)
Chicano students in a school incident.

Distributor Code [3]

A.D.F.   *American Documentary Films*
             336 West 84th Street
             New York, N.Y. 10024

B.   *Audio-Brandon Films, Inc.*

512 Burlington Avenue   8615 Directors Row
La Grange, Illinois 60525   Dallas, Texas 75247

34 MacQuesten Parkway, South 406 Clement Street
Mt. Vernon, New York 10550   San Francisco,
                              California 94101
1619 North Cherokee
Los Angeles, California 90028

B.U.S.D. *Berkeley United School District*

             BABEL
             1414 Walnut Street
             Berkeley, California 94701

C.   *Contemporary Films—McGraw Hill*

Eastern Office: Princeton Road
                   Hightstown, New Jersey 08520

Midwest Office: 828 Custer Avenue
                   Evanston, Illinois 60202

Western Office: 1714 Stockton Street
                   San Francisco, California 94133

---

[3] Because of frequent fluctuations in film rental fees, no prices are quoted. Current prices may be obtained from the nearest distributor at the time films are being ordered.

C.C.   *Centron Corporation*

           1621 West Ninth Street
           Lawrence, Kansas 66044

              Marketing Office: Suite 425
              1255 Post Street
              San Francisco, California 94109

C.F.W.C.   *Community Film Workshop Council, Incorporated*

           112 West 31st Street
           New York, N.Y. 10001

D.F.L.   *Donnell Film Library*

           20 West 53rd Street
           New York, N.Y. 10018

E.C.   *Espousal Center*

           554 Lexington Street
           Waltham, Massachusetts 02154

F.W.   *Film Wright*

           Diamond Heights, Box 31348
           San Francisco, California 94131

M.M.M.   *Mass Media Ministries*

           1720 Chouteau Avenue
           St. Louis, Missouri 63103

Part II: Films and Education for Cultural Pluralism [4]

Films and books are distinct and fundamentally different vehicles of communication. Trite and obvious though this statement may appear to be, it is of the utmost importance for teachers to bear in mind when

[4] By Anthony W. Hodgkinson, Associate Professor of Screen Education, Clark University and Worcester State College.

evaluating the usefulness, or otherwise, of the increasing number of films which present themselves for possible use in teaching within the context of cultural pluralism. Indeed, the difference between films and books is crucial in the teaching of any subject area.[5]

The reader of a book which aspires to present factual information and/or an intellectual argument has resources open to him denied to a film viewer. He can, at will, pause in his reading, check back to previous pages, consult other books or data, ponder the argument presented, seek elucidation by questions or discussion, and so on. Even if the book seeks, as in literature, to involve the reader emotionally, through devices such as narrative, dialogue, or descriptive passages, etc., the distance preserved between reader and book remains unviolated; emotional involvement and identification are subject both to the reader's skill in decoding the printed symbols and their conventions, and to his willingness to accept the author's intention.

Films are not read; they present the viewer with an experience as intense in many respects as the experience of actual reality, perhaps even more intense, since several experts suggest that film viewing approximates dreaming, an encounter with our own internal reality which, for all we know, may shape us more decisively than our waking experiences. Moreover, the film experience, even though an individual dream-like one, is rarely encountered alone. Others share the encounter with us; film viewing is normally a group experience. Part of our consciousness is of our fellow-audience, and our apprehension of their reactions to the group-dream becomes part of our total encounter, as do ours theirs.

Finally, a point of enormous importance for the teacher: The quality of the film experience is conditioned greatly by the context in which it takes place—whether, for example, as part of a classroom lesson, as a casual encounter at a movie house or on television, and so on. Introductory remarks (or their absence)—even the nature of the film's opening credits ("An Instructional Film by . . . ," contrasted to, say, "20th Century Fox Presents . . . ") set the viewer's mind on a certain track, provide him with a

---

[5] The special quality of the involvement between film and its viewers is in continuing process of examination. A recent and particularly valuable collection of short studies is contained in the April, 1971, issue of *The Journal of Aesthetic Education* (V, 2), published by the University of Illinois Press, Urbana, Illinois. Interested readers are recommended to this and may also obtain a bibliography of further studies from the Education Department of the American Film Institute, 1815 H Street N.W., Washington, D.C. 20006.

set of expectations related to previous experience, and condition his response to the film.

Many films produced with educational intent are themselves the results of failure on the part of their makers to appreciate some of the foregoing caveats. In the past especially, too many well-meaning "audio-visual aids to instruction" set out to emulate textbook forms; too many adaptations of "literature" were themselves overliteral and literary. In general, such films negated their own special filmic nature, and their use in both intellectual and emotional education was vitiated accordingly. In the preliminary choice of films for preview for the conference, attempts were made to exclude such examples. Fortunately, in the relatively recent framework for education which is "cultural pluralism," relevant films are generally of recent origin and do not share too many of these early basic faults of form and intention.

Yet, the pattern set in the minds of some teacher-viewers by a generation or more of falsely conceived "instructional films" may well have conditioned their response to some of those chosen. There may well have been a concern in some minds that insufficient "facts" were presented, insufficient intellectual argument produced, too "biased" a presentation made, and so on. Such demands from film are, in my view, wrongly conceived. But perhaps even more doubtful, to my mind, is the notion that worthwhile films can be relegated to a subordinate, "illustrative" role in relation to some intellectually defined "subject" which can be "taught."

The role of film in education is determined less by the nature of film than by the nature of education itself. If we conceive the essence of education as being instruction, as the imparting of factual data to, or training of, *tabula rasa* minds, then it may be valid to postulate "cultural plurality" as a subject area consisting of such data or skills, and to search for means whereby to convey them. Such means, in my view, are more likely to be books and book-like materials than true films. But if, as I have frequently argued,[6] the primary intent of education is the enlargement of the individual's awareness of himself and his role in human society, then film (and, indeed, all other arts) enters into its own as a creative force, a stimulus, a "dream machine," and a means of securing imaginative self-projection and identification with others. This last especially, I hope, is the intention which will motivate teaching when the concepts of cultural pluralism, as promulgated by this conference, are realized.

[6] See for example, my Report on the North Reading Screen Education Project (ERIC Document No. Ed 036205).